wym

enew by date shown.
. **norlink.norfolk.gov.uk**
)ne: **0344 800 8006**
library card & PIN ready.

D1580487

HAGGARD HAWKS AND PALTRY POLTROONS

HAGGARD HAWKS
AND
PALTRY POLTROONS

Paul Anthony Jones

Constable • London

Constable & Robinson Ltd
55-56 Russell Square
London WC1B 4HP
www.constablerobinson.com

First published in the UK by Constable,
an imprint of Constable & Robinson Ltd., 2013

A copy of the British Library Cataloguing in Publication
Data is available from the British Library

ISBN 978-1-4721-0806-7 (hardback)
ISBN 978-1-4721-0941-5 (ebook)

Printed and bound in the UK

1 3 5 7 9 10 8 6 4 2

For Phil, Matt and Arno

Acknowledgements

Any book of this nature is of course indebted to the scholars, lexicographers, compilers and wordsmiths from whose decades of work it is assembled. The material featured here has been pulled from a variety of different sources, but most notably the *Oxford English Dictionary* (still the single greatest scholarly achievement going) and the separate *Oxford Dictionary of Word Origins*; both the *Chambers Dictionary* and exceptional *Chambers Slang Dictionary*; *Brewer's Dictionary of Phrase & Fable*; and *Merriam-Webster's Collegiate Dictionary*. To all those involved in producing these exceptional titles I am immensely grateful.

Personal thanks to my agent, Andrew Lownie; to Hugh Barker at Constable; and to my parents, Leon and Maureen, for their unparalleled patience and proof-reading ability.

CONTENTS

CONTENTS

INTRODUCTION

Haggard is a strange word. Five centuries old, having been adopted into English from French in the mid-1500s, on its first appearance in the language it was a falconer's term used to refer to a wild hawk captured as an adult and then trained to hunt and retrieve prey. As these *haggard* hawks tended to remain quite wild and unpredictable even after their training, especially compared to captive-bred birds, over time the meaning of the word developed to come to describe anything similarly unruly, erratic, world-worn and – well, *haggard*. As unusual as this history is, however, *haggard* is not alone. It is just one of a number of English words, including *allure, turn-tail, rouse, poltroon* and even *codger,* that all share some kind of connection to falconry. And this is precisely what this book is all about.

Assembled here are fifty lists of ten words, each group of ten having some linguistic quality or etymological quirk in common. From words derived from places in Ancient Greece to words derived from colours, from unusual animal names to words with fictitious histories, and from *abbot, abdest* and *abelmosk* to *zed, zigzag* and *zombie,* the 500 entries listed in *Haggard Hawks and Paltry Poltroons* comprise some of the most remarkable words and word origins in the entire English language. Here you will find the connection between a family tree and a stork's foot, what connects a sitcom to a hybrid zebra, which item of gym equipment was originally a jailhouse punishment, what the first *blockbuster* was, how long an *ohnosecond* is, which weapon is named after a musical instrument, how to stop plagiarism with a spelling mistake, what you should really call a unknowledgeable critic, how to cure a fever with a magic word and where to find a vampire in a theatre. The entries here mix the familiar with the unfamiliar, the exceptional with the everyday, and the old with the new – you might not know what an *aphengescope* is, or how to *lucubrate*, but they are related to the chocolate éclair and the name of the shortest bone in your arm.

So, where better to begin than where the English language calls home . . .

I

TEN WORDS DERIVED FROM
PLACES IN BRITAIN

Besides the ten words listed in this chapter, the English language also contains a vast number of phrases and expressions that make reference to some British location, like *shipshape and Bristol fashion* and *carrying coals to Newcastle*. Expressions like these are often rooted in an area's association with a particular industry or historical event – *Bristol fashion* is derived from the city's world-renowned seafaring proficiency, while the naturally coal-rich north-east of England (as in WALLSEND) implies that *carrying coals to Newcastle* would be a thankless or pointless task. Likewise, to be *stabbed with a Bridport dagger* was a seventeenth-century phrase meaning to be 'hanged', referring to the rope-making industry of Bridport in Dorset; to *get yourself to Bath* was a nineteenth-century way of being told that you are talking nonsense, as the city's spring waters were once widely known to be used to treat patients with mental illnesses; and to walk *Newgate fashion* was a Shakespearean expression meaning to walk two-by-two, like prisoners shackled together in Newgate jail.

One of the most familiar of all of these British expressions, however, is also one of the most mysterious, as the origin of to *send to Coventry*, a seventeenth-century phrase meaning to 'ostracize' or 'ignore', is entirely unknown. Amongst the numerous suggestions attempting to explain its history are that it makes reference to a prison

1

established in the city during the Civil War; that the locals' supposed historical dislike of members of the British Army meant that anyone seen talking to a soldier would be shunned; or else that Coventry was once the site of an austere monastery, to which monks failing or disobeying their orders would have been sent to observe a strict vow of silence.

1. BADMINTON

The first recorded reference to the sport of *badminton* in English dates from 1863, when it was described as a game 'played with sides, across a string suspended some five feet off the ground'. Seemingly named after Badminton House, the Gloucestershire home of the Dukes of Beaufort, it is often claimed that the game originated amongst British Army officers on leave from India at Badminton in the nineteenth century. The game itself, meanwhile, is a development of the much earlier sixteenth-century game 'battledore and shuttlecock' (first recorded, rather unfortunately, as *shittle-cock* in the 1601 Ben Jonson play, *Cynthia's Revels*) in which two players, with no net between them, would attempt to bat a shuttlecock back and forth as many times as possible without letting it touch the ground.

2. BEDLAM

The word *bedlam*, describing a scene of utter madness or confusion, was first recorded in English in the mid-1600s. Derived from a corruption of *Bethlehem*, the word is ultimately taken from the name of the Hospital of St Mary of Bethlehem in London, a former thirteenth-century priory that was later converted into a hospital and, after the dissolution of the monasteries, into an insane asylum, hence its modern connotations. Indeed, the word is found as the name of an asylum in Shakespeare's *Henry VI, Part 2* (V. i), in which Lord Clifford dismisses Richard Plantagenet, the Duke of York's claim to the throne with the words, 'To Bedlam with him! Is the man grown mad?'

3. BORSTAL
As the name of a reformatory or detention centre for delinquent teenagers, the word *borstal* derives from the name of the village of Borstal near Rochester in north Kent, where just such an institution was established in 1902 on the site of an old Victorian prison. Used as a general term for any institution of this type since 1907, the word's very specific British origins have ultimately led to it being only seldom encountered outside of British English.

4. BRUMMAGEM
Brummagem is an old local name for the city of Birmingham and as such is the root of other familiar local words like *Brummie* and *Brum.* As an adjective, however, *brummagem* has been used since the mid-seventeenth century in English to describe anything inauthentic or counterfeit, as Birmingham once had a reputation across the country for the manufacture of counterfeit coinage. In the eighteenth and nineteenth centuries, the term came to be used more generally of anything showy yet cheaply made, and in particular referred to so-called *brummagem ware*, namely poor-quality metalwork or other merchandise of little real value.

5. CANTER
A horse's *canter* – that is, a slow to moderate galloping pace – derives its name from a shortening of *Canterbury,* the English ecclesiastical city in which the principal Archbishop of England and a famous shrine to St Thomas à Beckett are both located. Dating from the early

1600s, the term *canter* supposedly makes reference to the so-called 'Canterbury pace' or 'Canterbury trot', a colloquial name for the dawdling speed supposedly favoured by Christian pilgrims as they made their way to the city.

6. LYDDITE
Lyddite is an explosive, developed and widely employed by the British military in the late nineteenth century. First tested in 1888 – and named after the town of Lydd in Kent where the initial tests took place – *lyddite* was one of the first high explosives used in British mortar shells, produced by melting and then solidifying a volatile chemical known as trinitrophenol or picric acid. *Lyddite* was employed in both the Boer War and First World War until it began to be replaced by the relatively more reliable and controllable trinitrotoluene, better known as TNT, in the early twentieth century.

7. STRONTIUM
Chemical element number 38, *strontium* (Sr) is the only element of the periodic table named after a location in the British Isles. It derives its name from that of the Highland village of Strontian where its principal source mineral, strontianite, was first discovered in lead mines in the eighteenth century. A silvery-grey alkaline metal that is highly reactive to both water and oxygen, *strontium* was also one of the first elements to be isolated using electrolysis by the British chemist and inventor Sir Humphrey Davy in 1808.

8. SURREY
A *surrey* is a four-wheeled, two-seater American horse-drawn carriage so called as its design is believed to have developed from an earlier style of carriage first manufactured

in Surrey in the nineteenth century. Introduced to the United States in the 1870s, the first record of a *surrey* comes from the 1896 novella *An Open-Eyed Conspiracy* by the US writer William Dean Howells, but today the word is arguably much more familiar to English speakers thanks to the song 'The Surrey with the Fringe on Top', from the 1943 Rodgers and Hammerstein musical *Oklahoma!*

9. WALLSEND

Originally a town in Northumberland but now a suburb of the city of Newcastle upon Tyne, the place name *Wallsend* literally describes the town's location towards the eastern end of Hadrian's Wall. For over 150 years, from the end of the eighteenth century to the beginning of the twentieth century, the town was a major base for coal-mining in the north-east of England and was widely celebrated nationwide for the high quality of its produce – so much so, in fact, that the specific type of coal that the town produced came to be known as *Wallsend* in the early 1800s, as mentioned by Charles Dickens in *Our Mutual Friend*: 'I would rather have approached my respected father by candlelight . . . but we will take him by twilight, enlivened with a glow of Wallsend'.

10. WORSTED

Worsted is the name of both a type of yarn and a type of thick woollen fabric, both of which are thought to have been developed in the Norfolk village of Worstead by weavers and cloth-makers who emigrated to England from Flanders after the Norman Conquest. As the name of a fabric, the word was first recorded in English in the late thirteenth century, with the first reference to *worsted* yarn dating from the mid-fifteenth century.

II

TEN WORDS DERIVED FROM PLACES IN FRANCE

Unsurprisingly, a full list of English words originating in the names of French towns and cities would be dominated by culinary terms and the names of a great many foods and wines identified by their place of origin. Besides familiar examples like *champagne*, *Bordeaux* and *Dijon mustard*, however, are a number of much less familiar dishes: a *pithivier* is a rich puff-pastry tart of almond paste and cream, named after the town of Pithiviers outside Paris; a *plombière* is a dessert of glacé fruit and cream originally made in Plombières-les-Bains near Strasbourg; a *pavie* is a type of peach first grown in the town of the same name close to the Spanish border; and a *perigord* is a type of rich meat pie flavoured with truffles, originating in the Périgord region of the French south-west.

Outside of the kitchen, French place names are somewhat rarer in English, but are nevertheless encountered in the names of several different fabrics and textiles including DENIM, and, hinting at the country's mineral-rich geology, the names of a number of rocks and minerals, including BAUXITE, one of the most important minerals in the modern world.

I. ARTESIAN

The adjective *artesian* literally refers to the historical French province of Artois, now subsumed by the Pas-de-Calais department on France's north coast. In English, the term is most often encountered in reference to an *artesian well*, a method of accessing fresh water by drilling straight down into a water-rich layer of sloping rock beneath the ground, the raised angle of which maintains a constant pressure that pushes the water upwards through the well with little extra mechanical force required. The first recorded reference to an *artesian well* in English dates from the early nineteenth century, but this method of raising water is known to have been used throughout Artois since at least the Middle Ages.

2. BAUXITE

Bauxite is the chief commercial ore from which aluminium is obtained, making it arguably one of the most widely used ores in the world today. A dense, clayey rock typically containing a mixture of aluminium hydroxides, iron oxide and silica, *bauxite* takes its name from the town of Baux, or Les Baux-de-Provence, near Arles in the south of France, where rocks containing the mineral were first discovered by the French geologist Pierre Berthier in 1821.

3. BAYONET

Dating from the early 1600s in English, in its earliest sense the word *bayonet* described a short, flat pocket-dagger, but today it is generally only associated with the steel blade attached to the muzzle of a rifle or another similarly long-barrelled firearm, effectively turning it into a spear or pike. The origin of the word is uncertain, but it is likely that it is derived from the name of the French city of Bayonne, where blades like these were once presumably manufactured.

4. DENIM

Originally used for the name of a type of tough woollen fabric or serge, but now almost exclusively used to describe the thick cotton used to make jeans and other items, *denim* takes its name from the two-word French phrase *de Nîmes*, making mention of the city in the south of France where it was first made. *Denim* is just one of a number of textiles named from their French origins: *bewpers*, a cloth once used to make flags, comes from Beaupréau near Nantes; *lawn*, a type of linen, probably derives from the town of Laon in Picardy; *olderon*, a coarse fabric used to make sails, is thought to derive from Oléron, an island in the Bay of Biscay; and *shalloon*, a woollen fabric used as a lining cloth, derives from Châlons-en-Champagne in Marne, as does *chalon*, the name of a type of blanket or bed covering.

5. JURASSIC

The adjective *Jurassic* pertains to the period of geological history roughly 200 to 145 million years ago during which the dinosaurs flourished and early bird-like creatures began to evolve. Widely familiar in everyday English thanks to the popularity of the *Jurassic Park* film franchise, the term is derived from the name of the Jura Mountains, which straddle the border between France, Switzerland and Germany, and which are largely comprised of a form of limestone that characterizes the geological formations dating from this period. In English, the word *Jurassic* was first used in 1831, but in fact the term is known to have been coined somewhat earlier by the eighteenth- to nineteenth-century Prussian naturalist and explorer, Alexander von Humboldt.

6. LIMOUSINE

In English, the first use of the word *limousine* in reference to cars was recorded in 1902, when it applied specifically to a motor car comprising an open driver's seat and a separate, enclosed compartment for passengers. Before this, the term was purely used as an adjective referring to the Limousin region of central France. It is thought that when the first *limousine* cars were produced, the outer covering of the passenger compartment so resembled the hoods of Limousin shepherds that the word stuck and eventually evolved the meaning by which it is most familiar today.

7. MARTINGALE

In English, the word *martingale* dates from the early sixteenth century when it was first used as the name of a type of horse's harness, comprising a set of straps attached at one end around the girth and to the bit or noseband at the other, which was used to stop the horse from rearing up. In the nineteenth century, however, the term came to be used as the name of a type of betting system in which a losing player must double their stake in the hope that any future win would be great enough to offset all previous losses. In both contexts, *martingale* likely derives from *martengal*, an old French term for an inhabitant of Martigues, near Marseilles, which was originally used in French for the name of a type of breeches fastened around the waist and tied at the back, from where the horse's harness took its name. The connection between *martengal* and the *martingale* betting system, however, is unclear.

8. PICARDIE

In music, a *picardie* – or, more fully, a *tierce de Picardie*, or *Picardy third* – is the use of a major chord at the end of a piece of music that is otherwise written in a minor key, specifically a change made by raising a minor third (such as C and E-flat) by a semitone to a major third (C and E natural). Particularly associated with baroque music, this technique is also widely encountered in hymns and other religious music, as well as even in some pop and rock songs and traditional folk songs – the 'Coventry Carol' ('Lullay, lullay, Thou little tiny child'), for instance, has a familiar *picardie* ending. First described in English in the late seventeenth century, the origin of the term and quite why it should be named after the French region of Picardy are unknown, although it is popularly claimed that because this minor-to-major resolution is so prevalent in religious music, it may have simply originated amongst the innumerable churches and cathedrals of north-east France.

9. ROKELAY

A *rokelay* or *rocklay* is a type of women's cloak, typically short in length, which was popular in Europe during the eighteenth century. Although its derivation is unclear, it is likely that the word is related to the somewhat earlier term *roquelaure*, the name of a type of gentleman's cloak of considerably longer length and worn with a long, hanging collar. In turn, the *roquelaure* takes its name from that of a small village and duchy in the south-west of France whose local duke, Antoine-Gaston Jean Baptiste, an eighteenth-century Marshal of France, was supposedly a famous wearer of just such a garment.

10. TROY

The *troy* weight system, which is still used today as the standard system for weighing and measuring precious metals and gemstones, dates back as far as the late fourteenth century. Similar but not identical to the much more familiar imperial system (a *troy pound*, for instance, contains twelve ounces rather than sixteen), the *troy* system itself is of uncertain origin, but its name is believed to derive from the French market town of Troyes, south-east of Paris, where the system was presumably first used.

III

TEN WORDS DERIVED FROM PLACES IN ANCIENT GREECE

In linguistic terms, the impact of Ancient Greek on English is vast, despite the two languages historically having no direct contact. English is now home to many thousands of words derived at length from Ancient Greek roots, many of which have been adopted into English via French or Latin, or else have been deliberately coined from Greek sources by scientists and inventors. A full list of such coinages would include all *-phobias* (a term taken from the Greek word for 'fear', *phobos*) and all *-ologies* (from *logos*, meaning 'word') and *-isms* (from *ismos*, a Greek suffix used to form abstract nouns), plus a whole host of everyday words like *card* (*chartes*, 'paper, papyrus'), *history* (*historia*, 'study, learning through inquiry'), *bicycle* (*kuklos*, 'wheel, circle'), *diet* (*diaita*), *air* (*aer*) and *alphabet* (coined, appropriately enough, from the first two Greek letters, *alpha* and *beta*).

The ten words in this chapter have all been coined not from some distant Greek root word but instead from an Ancient Greek place name. Examples like these are rare in English and, as can be seen even from this short collection, many of those that do exist are fairly obscure (BOEOTIAN, LACONIC, SYBARITE), typically making reference to some characteristic once associated with a specific region of Greece. Nonetheless, alongside rarities like these, this list also includes an intriguing handful of

11

much more recognizable English words whose familiarity today belies their more exotic origins.

1. ATTIC

Use of the word *attic* as a noun denoting the topmost storey of a house is a surprisingly recent addition to the English language, dating from the early 1800s. Before then the term was a purely architectural one – an adjective used to describe a small decorative entablature or addition to the upper part of a column, or else a similarly decorative display or facade found above the main storey of a building, from where the modern sense of the word has since developed. Architectural features like these were once particularly associated with the Greek region of Attica, from where the term is originally derived.

2. BOEOTIAN

An unusual sixteenth-century word for a dullard or an ignorant, dim-witted person, the word *Boeotian* (pronounced 'bee-ocean') derives from the name of Boeotia, a central district of Greece just north of Athens, which was historically renowned for its supposedly stupid populace. This fairly derogatory association is believed to stem from the region's proximity to the much more cosmopolitan city of Athens, whose relatively cultured inhabitants presumably enjoyed looking down on their more rustic and unsophisticated neighbours to the north.

3. CHESTNUT

First recorded in English in the sixteenth century, the word *chestnut* (as well as the much earlier *chesteine*, an old-fashioned name for the chestnut tree itself) is believed to be derived from Castana, the name of a town in Thessaly where chestnuts were presumably once widely cultivated.

Like the brazil nut, however, it now seems likely that the town took its name from the nuts that grew there rather than the other way around, but either way the Latin term *castanea*, which is today used as the name of the genus to which chestnut trees belong, is generally taken to mean 'Castanian nut'.

4. CURRANT

The word *currant* dates from the fourteenth century, when the *raisins of Corauntz*, literally the 'raisins of Corinth', began to be sold in England for the very first time. As the name suggests, the fruits were once famously imported from Corinth in central Greece, and over time this name simply developed into the word as it is today. *Blackcurrants* and *redcurrants*, meanwhile, both derived their names from the English word *currant* in the early seventeenth century.

5. CYNICISM

Denoting a distrustful or sceptical attitude, the term *cynicism* derives from the Cynics of Ancient Greece, the followers of the fourth-century BC philosopher Antisthenes, who shunned power and wealth in favour of a simpler life of virtue, free of all worldly possessions. In turn, the Cynics are believed to have derived their name from that of the *Cynosarges*, a famous public gymnasium (an outdoor place of learning) on the outskirts of Athens, where Antisthenes is known to have once taught. According to legend, the *Cynosarges* itself is named after the Greek for 'white dog', *kynos argos*, as it was supposedly founded on the site of an ancient shrine built where a magnificent white dog dropped a chunk of meat it had stolen from a sacrificial offering.

6. LACONIC

Describing someone who is terse and economical in their speech, the term *laconic* derives from Laconia, the name of the southernmost region of mainland Greece that surrounded the city of Sparta. Indeed, the term in fact derives from the ancient Spartans themselves who were renowned for a similarly concise and direct disposition attested in several famous anecdotes recorded in ancient history. According to one story, when Philip II of Macedon set his sights on invading Sparta *c.*346 BC he sent a message reading 'If I enter your lands, I will destroy you all, never to rise again' to which the Spartans simply replied 'If'. Another Macedonian king, Demetrius I, also received a terse reply when he expressed outrage that Sparta had sent just one ambassador to attend his court – the envoy apparently replied, 'One ambassador, one king.'

7. LAODICEAN

Describing an apathetic or lukewarm attitude, especially towards religion, the unusual adjective *Laodicean* derives from the Ancient Greek region of Laodicea, now located in modern-day Turkey, whose inhabitants were once widely known for their religious indifference. So much so, in fact, that the Laodicean Church was one of the notoriously dissident Seven Churches of Asia mentioned by name in the biblical Book of Revelation, in which the book's author, John of Patmos, wrote decrying their nonchalant attitude: 'I know . . . that thou are neither cold nor hot, I would thou wert cold or hot. So, then because thou are lukewarm, and neither hot nor cold, I will spew thee out of my mouth.'

8. MAUSOLEUM

The original *mausoleum* from which all others take their name was the epic Mausoleum of Halicarnassus, the enormous tomb of Mausolus, a fourth-century BC ruler of the Ancient Greek province of Caria, which is today located in western Turkey. Erected by Mausolus's widow, Artemisia, this first *mausoleum* was one of a group of exceptional landmarks – alongside the Pyramids of Egypt and the Hanging Gardens of Babylon – chosen by the Greek poet Antipater of Sidon in the second century BC as one of the Seven Wonders of the Ancient World, a designation which undoubtedly helped to popularize the word *mausoleum* as a more general term for a tomb or resting place. In this sense, the word in English dates from the early 1500s.

9. SOLECISM

First recorded in the late sixteenth century, the word *solecism* is variously used to describe a grammatical or linguistic error, the improper use of language or of a particular word, or else, in a more figurative sense, a breach of good manners or etiquette. The term derives from the Greek word *soloikos*, meaning 'speaking incorrectly', which is itself thought to come from the name of Soli, a colony of Cilicia in the south of modern-day Turkey, whose populace were historically considered to speak a harsh and corrupted dialect of Greek by the more refined Athenians.

10. SYBARITE

A *sybarite* is a person devoted to the pursuit of pleasure or a lover of luxury and indulgence. Dating from the late 1500s in English, the term derives from the name of Sybaris, an Ancient Greek colony in what is now southern Italy, which flourished in the sixth and seventh centuries BC thanks to the remarkable fertility of its lands. As both the city and its wealth grew and grew, the lavishness that its inhabitants could afford became widely known and envied, and ultimately the name *sybarite* became synonymous with any equally decadent or hedonistic lifestyle.

IV

TEN WORDS DERIVED FROM
PLACES IN EUROPE

From the name of a global currency to a type of sword, and from an Adriatic sailing vessel to twentieth-century political terminology, the towns and countries of Europe – even excluding Britain, France and Greece, which each have their own chapters here – have provided the English language with a remarkably diverse collection of words and phrases, indicative of the continent's rich history. As well as BALKANIZATION, English has *Finlandization*, a 1960s political term describing a country's necessary but unfavourable support for another, derived from Finland's uneasy alignment with the Soviet Union in the 1940s. As well as COACH, English has both *landau*, an eighteenth-century horse-drawn carriage developed in Landau in Germany, and *Berlin*, a sixteenth-century four-wheeled carriage. And as well as RAMILLIES, English has *homburg*, a type of felt hat made in Homburg near the French-German border; *duffel*, from the Belgian town of Duffel, near Antwerp; and *jeans*, which take their name from the Italian city of Genoa. The stories behind ten more words of European etymology are listed here.

I. ARGOSY
A type of large merchant ship typically able to carry great loads, the word *argosy* derives from an alteration of *ragusea*, the Italian name for a type of vessel once

particularly associated with and named after the Adriatic port of Ragusa (now Dubrovnik) in Croatia. The word was first recorded in English in the late 1500s, and as well being the name of a specific type of ship is also used more generally for both a flotilla or fleet of vessels, and, figuratively, as another word for a vast collection or rich source of something.

2. BALKANIZATION
Dating from the 1920s, the political term *Balkanization* describes the breakup of a larger country or region into several smaller component nations, often with the implication that these smaller units remain equally hostile to one another. The word derives from the name of the Balkan peninsula of south-eastern Europe – the region bounded by the Adriatic, Aegean and Black Seas, which today includes the countries of the former Yugoslavia, Albania, Bulgaria and Greece. It originally referred to the uneasy dissolution of the European portion of the Ottoman Empire following the two Balkan Wars of 1912 and 1913. The aftermath of these conflicts, and the ensuing disagreements between the newly independent nations of Bulgaria, Albania, Serbia and Macedonia, eventually led to the assassination of Archduke Franz Ferdinand in Sarajevo in 1914, and ultimately to the First World War.

3. BILBO
The word *bilbo* has two meanings in English, applying both to a type of sixteenth-century sword with a flexible blade, once widely popular in America, and to a long iron bar fitted with shackles that is used to secure the ankles of prisoners. In both cases, the word is said to derive from the name of the Spanish city of Bilbao (once widely and

erroneously known in England as 'Bilboa') where both items are believed to have been first manufactured.

4. COACH

As the name of a type of carriage, the word *coach* was first recorded in English as *coche* in the mid-1500s. It derives via French from the Hungarian word *kocsi*, which is in turn taken from the name of the town of Kocs, roughly 50 km (30 miles) west of Budapest, where this style of carriage is thought to have first been manufactured in the fifteenth century. Use of the word *coach* to refer to a tutor or instructor, meanwhile, dates from the early nineteenth century and was originally an American slang term popular on university campuses, implying that a *coach* would 'carry' a failing student through their exams or studies.

5. DOLLAR

Now the name of the principal unit of currency of more than forty different countries and territories worldwide, the word *dollar* has its more humble beginnings in Jáchymov, a small Bohemian spa town today located in the Czech Republic close to the German border. Previously known as Joachimsthal, in the early 1500s the town gave its name to coins known as *joachimsthaler*, widely used across Germany and the Netherlands, which were minted from silver mined nearby. Over time, the name shortened to *thaler*, *taler* and *daler* (by which they were first mentioned in English in 1553), and eventually to *dollar* in the early 1700s. The word first appeared in North America in the late 1500s as another name for the peso or so-called 'Spanish dollar', the former currency of Spain and its American colonies, but it was not until 1785 that *dollar* was first used as the name of the currency of the United States. The dollar sign ($), meanwhile, is thought to have developed either from a combination of the letters P and S, a symbol once used to denote the peso, or else from the number 8, as pesos were the original *peso de ocho* or 'pieces of eight'.

6. DONNYBROOK

Dating from the mid-nineteenth century in English, the word *donnybrook* is another name for a riotous argument or uproar. The word derives from the Irish village of Donnybrook or *Domhnach Broc* ('The Church of St Broc'), now a suburb of the city of Dublin, where from the early thirteenth century to the mid-nineteenth century an annual two-week agricultural fair and farmers' market was held every August. Originally granted its licence by King John in 1204, over the centuries that followed the event grew increasingly unruly, with various rowdy and bawdy entertainments provided for its visitors. Despite several attempts to cancel it in the eighteenth century – the Mayor of Dublin himself even demanded that all of the stalls and tents be torn down in 1751 – the fair's original royal permit remained valid, and it was not until the 1850s, when a local reverend raised £3,000 to purchase the licence from its holders, that the fair was finally discontinued. It was last held in 1854.

7. RAMILLIES

The Belgian town of Ramillies, around 40 km (25 miles) south-east of Brussels, has given its name to a number of obsolete items of fashion, all of which are said to derive from or commemorate the Duke of Marlborough's victory over the French at the Battle of Ramillies in 1706. The earliest mention to the town in this context is in the name of the *ramillies cock*, a type of hat with a wide brim cocked in three places that was popular in the early 1700s, but the name can also be used to refer to a type of wig tied back in a long, tapering plait, known as a *ramillies tail*, fastened with a large bow at the top and a smaller bow at the bottom.

8. SEMTEX
A type of plastic explosive used both in demolition and by the military, *Semtex* was invented in 1966 by a Czechoslovakian chemist named Stanislav Brebera at a chemical production plant in Semtín (now in the Czech Republic), from where the name is said to be derived. First recorded in English in a *New York Times* article of 1985, in recent years *Semtex* has become increasingly associated with terrorist activities, and was infamously used to destroy Pan Am Flight 103 over Lockerbie in 1988.

9. SPA
The original *spa* from which all others have since taken their name is the small town of Spa in Liège, eastern Belgium; a spring of fresh water with supposed natural healing properties, situated in the town, has been known throughout Europe since the fourteenth century. Deriving its name from a local Walloon word, *espa*, meaning 'spring' or 'fountain', the word *spa* was first recorded in English in reference to a site of similarly curative waters in 1616, and from the mid-seventeenth century onwards has been used more loosely for any town or resort with local natural springs. Use of the word to refer to a commercial health farm, meanwhile, originated in the United States in the 1960s.

10. WATERLOO
One of the most important battles in all of European history, it was at Waterloo on 18 June 1815 that Napoleon

was finally defeated by a united British and Prussian force under the command of the Duke of Wellington. Whilst today the village of Waterloo itself stands in central Belgium, just a few miles south of Brussels, at the time of the conflict it stood within the borders of the Netherlands. Indeed, the name *Waterloo* is believed to be of Dutch origin and is said to mean 'wet forest', presumably in reference to a boggy or flood-prone area of land. Given the battle's great historical importance, it is perhaps unsurprising that the word *Waterloo* has since slipped into allusive use in the English language as a byword for any similarly decisive event or else some great insurmountable difficulty or defeat – in fact, the first recorded use of the word in this context dates from just one year after the battle itself, when it appeared in the writings of the English poet Lord Byron, who commented on his attempt to learn Armenian that, 'It is a rich language, however . . . It is a Waterloo of an alphabet.'

V

TEN WORDS DERIVED FROM PLACES IN AMERICA

Probably the most famous of all American place names to have crept into the English language is *Hollywood*, which has been used as a byword for the American film industry since the early 1920s. Now a district of downtown Los Angeles, Hollywood was originally an agricultural ranch established by the Kansan real estate agent Harvey H. Wilcox in 1886 and named by his wife, Daeida. When Wilcox began selling off barns and other large outbuildings on his land to movie producers for use as film studios in the late 1800s, Hollywood's association with the cinema was born. The famous Hollywood sign, meanwhile, was erected in 1923 as a real estate promotion and originally read 'Hollywoodland'.

I. BOURBON

Produced since the eighteenth century and first recorded in English in the mid-1800s, *bourbon* whiskey takes its name from Bourbon County, one of the oldest counties in the state of Kentucky. In turn, the county takes its name from that of the French royal house of Bourbon, the dynasty that ruled France from the late sixteenth century through to the abolition of the monarchy after the French Revolution in 1792. The county, and hence the drink, was supposedly named in honour of King

Louis XVI's support of the American cause during the War of Independence.

2. BUNKUM

Meaning 'nonsense' or 'rubbish', the word *bunkum* was first recorded in English in the early nineteenth century and is derived from an infamous event in American politics in which the US Congressman Felix Walker, representative of Buncombe County in North Carolina, delivered a long and rambling speech to the House of Representatives in February 1820. According to the story, Congress had already been debating the so-called Missouri Question – that is, whether to admit Missouri to the Union as a free or slave state – for quite some time when, just before the decisive vote was due to be called, Walker stood to address the House. With his already exasperated colleagues keen to conclude the debate, Walker was implored not to continue but regardless went on to deliver a dull, lengthy and wholly unnecessary speech, which is believed to have had no real intention other than simply making headlines back home – 'I shall not be speaking to the House,' Walker famously explained, 'but to Buncombe.' This memorable explanation soon caught on in American political slang, and 'talking for Buncombe' or 'making a pass for Buncombe' both became popular catchphrases in the 1830s. Eventually, the word itself came to be used as a general term for nonsense or waffling talk in the 1860s, with the abbreviated form *bunk* developing around 1900, and the verb *debunk* first recorded in 1923.

3. CHARLESTON

The name of the *Charleston*, a lively dance popular in the 1920s in which the legs are kicked swiftly outwards from the knee, was first recorded in the title of a piece of popular music composed in 1923 by the American pianist James P. Johnson and the lyricist Cecil Mack – supposedly, Johnson took his inspiration for the piece from the music of the black dock-workers of Charleston, South Carolina, from where it takes its name. Originally written for a Broadway show, the song's popularity soon spread throughout the United States, and both it and the dance craze it inspired went on to become one of the most iconic symbols of the decade.

4. CHAUTAUQUA

Seldom encountered outside of North American English, a *chautauqua* is an educational summer exposition or assembly, typically held outdoors and featuring lectures and classes on various subjects as well as concerts, plays and other entertainments. The term dates from the 1870s and derives from an original series of summer schools and classes organized amongst the Methodist community of the town and county of Chautauqua in the west of New York state, which were first held in 1874. The place name itself, meanwhile, is thought to be of Iroquoian origin.

5. HOOCH

As a slang term for alcohol – and especially homemade or poor-quality alcohol – the word *hooch* was first recorded in English in the late nineteenth century and derives from the name of a tribe of Tlingit Native Americans, known as the Hoochinoo, who were based on Admiralty Island in the far south-east of Alaska. The tribe, who were known for selling their own homemade liquor to prospectors during the American Gold Rush, in turn took their name from a local Tlingit word meaning 'grizzly bear fort', and so the word presumably first referred to a settlement on the island, which is indeed home to the densest population of brown bears in the whole of North America.

6. MONADNOCK

Also known as an *inselberg* (from the German for 'island mountain'), in geology a *monadnock* is an isolated peak or ridge that rises up sharply out of an otherwise flat expanse of land. Typically formed from more resistant rock than its surroundings, the *monadnock* is simply revealed over time as its neighbouring rocks are eroded and washed away. The term was first used in English in the late nineteenth century and was borrowed directly from the name of Mount Monadnock in New Hampshire, which is a prime example of a peak of this type. The mountain's name itself is believed to be a corruption of *menonadenak*, a word taken from the native Abenaki language of the north-east United States, which literally means 'smooth mountain'.

7. PINHOOKER

First recorded in 1885, *pinhooker* is an old American slang term for a profiteer or speculator who typically purchases a commodity cheaply with the intention of later selling it on for profit. Originally used in relation to tobacco, today the term is chiefly associated with racehorses, and often pertains to the practice of buying young thoroughbred horses as yearlings with the expectation that a profit can be made once they are fully grown. Although the origins of the word are questionable, it is often claimed that it derives from the tiny town of Bratton's Mill in Kentucky, which was once reportedly known as Pinhook: in American regional slang, a *pinhook town* is a nickname for a remote rural settlement so called as the locals supposedly make their own fishing hooks from nails and pins.

8. POCOSIN

A *pocosin* is a marsh or bog, and in particular refers to low-lying marshland in an otherwise dry and upland or wooded area. First recorded in English in the mid-seventeenth century, the term is thought to be of Algonquian origin and is likely descended from the name of a tidal river in Virginia, the Poquoson, which forms an inlet of Chesapeake Bay on the United States' Atlantic coast.

9. TUXEDO

First recorded in 1889 (with the abbreviation *tux* dating from 1922) the *tuxedo* dinner jacket takes its name from New York's Tuxedo Park, the site of a well-known country club where it is popularly claimed that the short, tailless *tuxedo* jacket was first worn in the mid-1880s. The place name *Tuxedo* itself, meanwhile, is thought to come from the language of the native Lenape Americans, whose name for the area, *tucseto*, supposedly meant 'clear flowing water'.

10. TEXAS

The *texas* is the uppermost section or deck of a southern American steamboat or paddle steamer, often the section of the boat that contains the officers' quarters and pilot-house. Dating from the mid-1800s, the term apparently originates in the practice of naming the cabins and decks of Mississippi river vessels after various states – as the officers' quarters typically contained the largest cabins, the name was simply taken from what was at the time the largest state in the Union.

VI

TEN BRITISH WORDS NOT USED IN AMERICAN ENGLISH

Differences between American and British English can be seen on almost every linguistic level, with the two varieties differing in their phonology, their grammar and phrasing, their spelling and punctuation, and their vocabulary. Listed in this chapter are the stories behind ten words familiar to speakers of British English that have, for one reason or another, failed to gain little recognition in North America.

This is not to say that British English has embraced much in the way of American vocabulary in return, as besides shunning the vast majority of spelling reforms popularized by the nineteenth-century American lexicographer Noah Webster (like *color, encyclopedia* and *catalog*), British English steadfastly prefers *skirting-board* to *baseboard, pharmacy* to *drugstore, pushchair* to *stroller,* and *turnip, spring onion, rocket* and *courgette* to the America *rutabaga, scallion, arugula* and *zucchini.* Even some American terms like *gasoline* (1860s), *pacifier* (1901) and *elevator* (1780s) have never been fully adopted into British English despite predating their British equivalents *petrol* (1890s), *dummy* (1907) and *lift* (1850s), whilst even some words that British speakers would consider obvious Americanisms were in fact originally used in Britain but have simply fallen out of use. The word *faucet,* for instance, dates back as far as the fifteenth century when

28

it was originally applied to a tap or plug used to drain alcohol from a barrel, and similarly *diaper* (1600s), *candy* (1650s), *sidewalk* (1660s), *railroad* (1750s) and *tailpipe* (1880s) were all originally British terms that have simply vanished from the language.

1. BOFFIN

Almost entirely exclusive to British English, the word *boffin* is today used as a humorous name for a scientist or intellectual, but on its first appearance in the language in the early 1940s was originally used in the Armed Forces, and in particular the RAF, as a slang term for an older and more experienced officer. The origin of the word is unclear, but given the prevalence of earlier English literary characters named *Boffin* – such as those found in Tolkien's *The Hobbit*, and the character of Noddy Boffin in Dickens's *Our Mutual Friend* – it is likely that the name was at some point pilfered from one of these.

2. CROTCHET

Dating from the fifteenth century and taking its name from an old hook-shaped implement which it apparently resembles, in British musical notation a *crotchet* is a single note equal to one full beat; its American counterpart is the *quarter note*, so called as it is equal to one-quarter of a *whole note* or British *semibreve*. Indeed, most musical notes are known by different names in British and American English: the *minim*, equal to two beats, is known as a *half note* in America; the *quaver* and *semiquaver*, one-half and one-quarter of a beat respectively, are otherwise known as *eighth* and *sixteenth notes*; and, beyond these, the *demisemiquaver* (half the value of a *semiquaver*) and *hemidemisemiquaver* (half the value again) are, in the American system, known as *thirty-second* and *sixty-fourth notes*. That is not to say that either of these systems is the 'correct' or 'proper' one, however, as the differences between the two simply reflect their distinct origins – the British names are descended from the original Italian terms, whilst the arithmetical arrangement favoured by American English is a translation of the system used in German.

3. FORTNIGHT

Derived from the Old English *feowertyne niht*, literally meaning 'fourteen nights', as surprising as it may seem to British English speakers to whom the word is so familiar, American English has never truly embraced the word *fortnight*. Quite why the word remains something of an oddity in American English is unclear, although it seems all the more unusual given its prevalence not only in British English but also in the vocabularies of many other English-speaking nations including Australia and New Zealand, and parts of Canada, India and Pakistan. The obsolete term *sennight*, meanwhile, describing a period of seven nights, has all but vanished from all varieties of English.

4. GORMLESS

Meaning 'slow-witted', the adjective *gormless* is thought to have existed as a British dialect term long before its first recorded written use in Emily Brontë's *Wuthering Heights* in 1847. Rarely encountered in American English, the term remains an almost uniquely British word, thought to be derived from some long-obsolete Middle English term, *gome* or *gawm*, which would have presumably meant 'notice' or 'attentiveness'. As this Middle English form has no equivalent in Modern English, *gormless* is also an example of a so-called 'unpaired' word, namely one which despite appearances does not have an opposite

30

counterpart, like *disgruntled, disambiguate, uncouth* and *ruthless.*

5. JIGGERY-POKERY

The colloquialism *jiggery-pokery*, meaning 'manipulation' or 'deceit', is one of several nonsense-sounding British words which are rarely, if ever, encountered in American English. It was probably adopted into English from Scottish – the seventeenth-century equivalents *joukery-pawkery* and *jewkrypawkry* are likely built around the Scots word *jouk*, meaning to 'dodge' or 'swerve'. Similar examples of nonsense-sounding words include the nineteenth-century term *argy-bargy* or *argle-bargle*, meaning 'an argument'; *skew-whiff*, dating from the eighteenth century and meaning 'off centre' or 'awry'; and *shilly-shally*, an eighteenth-century expression meaning to 'waste time' or 'procrastinate', thought to be a playful variation of the phrase 'shall I?'

6. SECATEURS

Known simply as 'pruning shears' in American English, the word *secateurs* is based on a French loanword, *sécateur*, which was adopted into British English in the late 1800s. Ultimately descended from the Latin verb *secare*, meaning 'to cut' (from which words like *dissect, intersect* and *sector* are all also derived), the word was originally singular but is now always used as a plural in English, its etymologically unnecessary final 's' having been added through association with similar words like *scissors* and *shears* in the early twentieth century.

7. TITCHY

Meaning 'very small', the word *titchy* is a relatively recent British coinage derived from the nickname of the nineteenth- to twentieth-century London-born entertainer Harry Relph, who performed under the stage name of Little Tich. The popularity of Tich (who stood just four-foot-six tall) in the early 1900s eventually led to his character's name being more widely applied to any similarly diminutive person or child, and ultimately to the invention of the adjective *titchy* as recently as the 1950s. Due to the somewhat specific association with British music hall culture, *titchy* simply never caught on in American English.

8. TWEE

As an adjective meaning 'quaint' or 'dainty', the chiefly British word *twee* dates from the early twentieth century, and is believed to be formed from an intentionally childish pronunciation of the word 'sweet'. First used genuinely with real affection or intention, the word has developed a more depreciative meaning over time and today tends only to be applied to things that are mawkish or over-affectedly sweet.

9. WHINGE

Meaning 'whine' or 'moan', the verb *whinge* is a surprisingly old British word dating from the twelfth century and thought to originate in the dialects of Scotland and northern England. The word *maunder*, also of dialect origin and similarly meaning 'grumble' or 'dawdle', is likewise exclusively used in British English, whilst the Americanisms *bellyache* and *kvetch*, both meaning 'complain' or else a 'person who habitually finds faults', are found much less frequently in British English.

10. ZED

In modern British English, the last letter of the alphabet is known as *zed* while in American English it tends to be called *zee*. Historically, however, both *zed* and *zee* were used interchangeably in both British and American English, alongside a whole host of other more outlandish names for Z including *izzard, shard, ezod* and *uzzard*, all of which have long since fallen out of use. Of the two, *zed* is the earlier, derived at length from the name of the equivalent Greek letter *zeta* and first attested in written English in the fifteenth century. *Zee*, meanwhile, was first recorded in the seventeenth century in a British English spelling book and is thought to have originated as a dialect variation of *zed* probably influenced by the regular *bee, cee, dee, ee* pattern of much of the rest of the alphabet. Quite how or why *zee* became the dominant form in American English is unclear, but it has been suggested that because *zed* tended to be favoured by British speakers, during the Revolution and America's fight for independence in the late eighteenth century American English speakers would have wanted to distance themselves from anything even vaguely suggestive of Great Britain and hence adopted *zee* in preference.

VII

TEN WORDS BORROWED FROM UNUSUAL LANGUAGES

As much as 80 per cent of all English words can be categorized by their etymology into one of just three original sources: Germanic, Latin and French. Despite English itself being classed as a Germanic language (Anglo-Saxon evolved from the same ancient, unrecorded language of north-central Europe as German and Dutch), the Germanic group is actually the smallest of these three, yet includes some of the most basic and frequently used of all words that have been retained in the language since the Old English period, like *town, eye, stone* and *tree*, plus function words like *the, and, on* and *that.* Latin, meanwhile, was once the language of the law (*legislation, jurisprudence*), the Church (*monk, priest, altar*) and education, and hence Latin-origin words tend to be characterized by a great many more formal and technical terms. In contrast, a full list of French-origin words – which may comprise as much as 30 per cent of the language – would be dominated by political (*sovereign, government, mayor*), legal (*court, case, jury*), military (*sergeant, infantry, brigade*) and cultural terms (*cuisine, aisle, arch*) adopted into the language after the Norman Conquest.

Most of the remainder of English comprises a hotch-potch of other etymological sources – including Ancient Greek, ancient British and Celtic languages, proper names, acronyms and compounds of existing words – whilst around 5 per cent comprises loanwords adopted more recently from other languages, many of which have been absorbed into English as it has spread around the globe. Ten examples of loanwords borrowed from some fairly obscure source languages are listed here.

1. ANORAK

The name of a type of thick, usually hooded waterproof jacket, the word *anorak* is one of only a handful that English has borrowed from the Inuit languages of the Arctic. It comes from the language of the native Greenlanders, whose term *annoraaq* is used to describe a waterproof coat typically made of animal hide. Besides a handful of other familiar words like *igloo* and *kayak*, the majority of other Inuit-origin words in English are somewhat obscure and have very specific applications, like *aglu*, an Eskimo word for a breathing-hole cut into ice by a seal; *komatik*, a type of dogsled used by the Inuit of Canada's Labrador Island; *nunatak*, a Greenlandic word for an peak of rock projecting above an expanse of ice; and *qiviut*, an East Canadian Inuit word for the wool of the musk ox.

2. BATIK

First recorded in English in the mid-nineteenth century, *batik* is a traditional south-east Asian art form in which a canvas or fabric is partly covered in wax and then dyed so that the wax-covered areas are left uncoloured, the process typically being repeated with several different colours to create remarkably complex designs. Believed to have been first introduced into Britain via the Netherlands, the process originated in the former Dutch colony of Java in Indonesia, and as such *batik* – literally meaning 'painted' – is one of only a handful of Javanese words used in English. Of similar origin are the names of several animals (including the *banxring*, a small squirrel-like mammal), musical instruments (*gamelan*, a percussion instrument) and foods (*gado-gado*, a type of vegetable salad), all of which are native to Java.

3. BOONDOCK
Used to describe any remote or wild place – and hence *boondockers* are heavy shoes suitable for such rough terrain – the word *boondock* (from *bundok*, meaning 'mountain') was adopted into English from Tagalog, the official language of the Philippines, by American troops who occupied the islands in the early 1900s. The word is one of very few that Tagalog has contributed to the language, the majority of which tend to be the names of native Filipino animals and plants such as the *malmag*, a type of tarsier; *cogon*, a type of grass; *buri*, a type of palm; and *ylang-ylang*, a tree from which a much prized perfumed oil is obtained.

4. CHOCOLATE
English has adopted a remarkably familiar collection of words from the indigenous languages of North America, including such terms as *moccasin, tomato, hickory, raccoon, toboggan, avocado* and, predictably, both *wigwam* and *tepee*. Of all words to have their origins in the early Americas, however, perhaps the most surprising is *chocolate*, which was borrowed into English via Spanish in the early seventeenth century. Although the precise origins of the word are debatable, it is thought that it is derived from the language of the Aztecs, Nahuatl, whose word *xocolatl* was used for a chocolaty drink made from the seeds of the cacao tree.

5. KAHUNA

Kahuna is one of just a few words that English has adopted from Hawaii, where, historically, the word was originally used for a priest or wise man. First recorded in English in the late nineteenth century, in the twentieth century the word was somewhat humorously taken on by surfers as a name for the 'god' of the waves, and by the 1950s the phrase *big kahuna* had become a popular slang term for a particularly skilled surfer. The more general use of the word, a 'person of importance', dates from the 1960s.

6. OMBUDSMAN

Historically derived from the Old Norse word *umbuðs-mann*, 'one who acts on behalf of another', the word *ombudsman* was adopted into English from Swedish in the 1870s. Like its historical counterpart, the modern use of the word derives from the position of Parliamentary Ombudsman, or *justitieombudsman*, a representative in the Swedish parliament employed to investigate complaints against the state by the people. The word is easily one of the most recognizable of all Swedish words used in English – alongside others like *moped*, *nickel* and *smorgasbord* – with some of the less familiar examples including *lek*, the breeding display of grouse and other game-birds; *glögg*, a drink of warmed, sweetened and spiced wine and brandy; and *fartlek*, literally meaning 'speed play', a method of cross-country athletics training in which runners alternate between a fast and slow pace.

7. PARIAH

Used in English since the eighteenth century for an outcast or recluse, in its earliest sense the word *pariah* referred to a ceremonial drummer at rituals held amongst the lowest castes of India, and indeed the word itself is derived from the Tamil word for 'drum'. As members of these castes, especially during British rule in India, were often employed as servants, labourers and in other equally humble positions, eventually the term *pariah* came to be more widely associated with all members of India's lowest castes, from where the modern use of the word has since developed. Tamil-origin words are rare in English, but amongst a handful of other examples is *catamaran*, which derives from the Tamil *katta-maram*, the name of a type of simple raft made from two logs roped together.

8. SAUNA

Although the word itself is much older, *sauna* was first recorded in English in 1881. It is one of very few words that English has adopted from Finnish, and is by far the most familiar, with the remaining examples including some very rare and specific words indeed: a *pulka* is a single-man sledge pulled by a reindeer; *rapakivi* is the name of a form of granite; a *puukko* is a traditional Finnish knife with a curved blade; and a *kantele* is a type of Finnish zither with a characteristic bell-like sound.

9. TABOO

The word *taboo* is derived from Tongan, the language of the Kingdom of Tonga lying almost 2,000 km (1,360 miles) north-east of New Zealand. First attested in the journals of Captain Cook written whilst on his voyage to the Pacific Ocean in 1777, as Cook explained in his original notes the word is 'of very comprehensive meaning', but in general describes anything 'forbidden'. Similar words of almost identical meaning are found in a whole host of languages across Polynesia, including in New

Guinea, Kiribati and Micronesia (*tapu*), Hawaii (*kapu*), Fiji and the Solomon Islands (*tambu*).

10. TUNDRA

First recorded in English in the mid-1800s, *tundra* is perhaps the only word found in English today to have been derived from the Saami languages of the northernmost regions of Scandinavia and north-west Russia. Used to describe the flat, treeless expanses of open land that cover Siberia (and, by extension, North America and Greenland), *tundra* is specifically thought to originate in Kildin, a remarkably rare and increasingly endangered language spoken by just a few hundred people inhabiting Russia's Kola Peninsula on the White Sea.

VIII

TEN WORDS INVENTED BY SHAKESPEARE

After the Bible and *The Times* newspaper, William Shakespeare is the third most quoted source in the entire *Oxford English Dictionary* (OED), with his works providing almost twice as many citations as the next most-quoted author, Sir Walter Scott, and more than three times as many as Charles Dickens. Shakespeare accounts for just over 33,000 references in the OED (5 per cent of which are from *Hamlet* alone) of which some 1,500 provide the first recorded use of a word in the English language, and a further 8,000 provide the first record of an existing word being used in a new sense or context. Although it cannot be said that Shakespeare personally created all of these new words and senses (his works merely provide their first written evidence), nonetheless his linguistic creativity is clear.

Listed here are the stories behind ten Shakespearean coinages, from words as deceptively modern as ADVERTISING and WATCHDOG, to more bookish terms like BOSKY and LACKLUSTRE. His use of ELBOW in *King Lear*, meanwhile, is a prime example of his inventive adaptation of a pre-existing English word.

1. ADVERTISING

Admittedly, Shakespeare's use of the word *advertising* – 'as I was then / Advertising and holy to your business / . . . I

40

am still / Attorney'd at your service' (*Measure for Measure*, V. i) – does not bear the same sense of the word we use today, but instead points to a much earlier use of the verb *advertise*, dating from the fifteenth century, to mean to 'warn' or 'call attention to' or 'take notice of'; Shakespeare's *advertising* is in fact an adjective, essentially meaning 'watchful' or 'attentive'. Derived from an Old French verb *avertir* meaning 'to become aware of', this early meaning of *advertise* gradually developed to come to mean 'make known' or 'give public notice', from where the modern sense of the word implying commercial promotion or publicity eventually derived in the eighteenth century.

2. AMAZING

As an adjective, the first recorded use of the word *amazing* in English is recorded in Shakespeare's *Richard II* (I. iii), in which John of Gaunt rousingly exclaims 'And let thy blows . . . / Fall like amazing thunder on the casque / Of thy adverse pernicious enemy'. Thought to be derived from some unknown Old English word, *mase* or *maze*, meaning 'confusion' or 'delirium', the word *amazing* originally meant 'terrifying' or 'dreadful' and was used to describe anything that stupefies or overwhelms. It was not until the eighteenth century that it began to apply to anything astounding or wondrous, the sense by which it is most often used today.

3. ASSASSINATION

Fittingly, the word *assassination* was first used in English in Shakespeare's *Macbeth* (I. vii), in a soliloquy delivered by Macbeth himself in which he mulls over the proposed murder of King Duncan and its aftermath: 'If the assassination / Could trammel up the consequence, and catch / With his surcease success; that but this blow / Might be the be-all and the end-all here'. The word is formed around the earlier *assassin*, first recorded in English in the early 1500s, which is itself thought to be descended from an Arabic word meaning 'hashish-eaters', *hashishin*, once used for members of a radical Muslim sect known for intoxicating themselves with hashish before carrying out the murders of rival leaders or public figures.

4. BAREFACED

First recorded in Shakespeare's *A Midsummer Night's Dream* (I. ii) – 'Some of your French crowns have no hair at all, and then you will play bare-faced' – the earliest use of the word *barefaced* in English was a literal one, meaning simply 'unmasked' or 'with the face uncovered'. Also used in both *Hamlet* (IV. v) and *Macbeth* (III. i), the word gained its broader and more familiar use, meaning 'audacious' or 'impudent', in the eighteenth century, the sense by which it appears in Dickens's *Oliver Twist*: 'Of all the artful and designing orphans . . . you are one of the most bare-facedest'.

5. BOSKY

The odd word *bosky* was first recorded in Shakespeare's *The Tempest* – 'My bosky acres and my unshrubbed down' (Iv. i) – where it is used to mean 'bushy' or 'covered in vegetation'. It is derived from the Old English dialect word *bosk*, referring to a bush or thicket, with the addition of the suffix -*y* to form an adjective. Other words Shakespeare coined in this way include *doughy* (in *All's Well That Ends Well*, IV. v), *leaky* (*The Tempest*, I. i, and *Antony and Cleopatra*, III. xiii), *beachy*, in the sense of 'covered by a beach' (*Henry IV, Part 2*, III. i), *barky*, meaning 'bark-covered' (*A Midsummer Night's Dream*, IV. i), and *shelvy,* meaning 'of different levels' (*The Merry Wives of Windsor,* III. v).

6. DAUNTLESS
The adjective *dauntless* was first recorded in Shakespeare's *Henry VI, Part 3* (III. iii) – 'Let thy dauntless mind still ride in triumph, over all mischance'. Formed from the earlier verb *daunt,* adapted from the Old French *danter* meaning 'to subdue' or 'to tame', the word is one of a number of familiar adjectives featuring the suffix *-less* that were first recorded in Shakespeare's works: *countless* is used in his 1593 poem *Venus and Adonis; airless* is found in the opening act of *Julius Caesar* (I. iii); *noiseless* was first used in *King Lear* (IV. ii) and reappeared in *All's Well that Ends Well* (V. iii); and *priceless* was used in his epic poem *The Rape of Lucrece*: 'What priceless wealth the heavens had him lent / In the possession of his beauteous mate'.

7. ELBOW
To say that Shakespeare himself coined the word *elbow* is incorrect, as the word was already several centuries old before his time. What Shakespeare is responsible for, however – as is the case with several words to which he is attributed – is the adaption of the noun *elbow* into a verb, meaning to 'nudge' or 'jostle out of the way'; the term appears in *King Lear* (IV. iii), in the phrase 'A sovereign shame so elbows him'. Amongst the many other nouns Shakespeare similarly transformed into verbs are *cake, hinge, lapse, cater, torture, choir, attorney, cudgel, bet, sire, canopy* and *rival.*

8. LACKLUSTRE
The word *lacklustre* first appeared in Shakespeare's *As You Like It* (II. vii), in which the melancholy Jacques recalls a

meeting in the forest with Touchstone, the clown, who 'drew a dial from his poke, / And, looking on it with lacklustre eye, / Says very wisely, "It is ten o'clock"'. This same speech is also the origin of the phrase 'and thereby hangs a tale', whilst the well-known expressions 'too much of a good thing' (IV. i), 'neither rhyme nor reason' (III. ii), 'forever and a day' (IV. i) and 'laid on with a trowel' (I. ii) have all been taken from *As You Like It*.

9. UNSEX

Shakespeare coined the unusual verb *unsex* for use in *Macbeth* (I. v), in which Lady Macbeth exclaims, 'Come, you spirits / That tend on mortal thoughts! Unsex me here, / And fill me from the crown to the toe full / Of direst cruelty', pleading that she may have her feminine attributes removed so that she would be able to carry out the masculine act of murder. The word essentially means to 'remove the sexual characteristics of someone', but it could also be taken to mean to 'disguise' or 'hide the characteristics of', and has since been used more figuratively by other writers to mean to 'distort' or 'make ugly'. Other *un-* verbs coined by Shakespeare include *uncheck* (*Timon of Athens*, IV. iii), *unhand* (*Hamlet*, I. iv), *unbless* (Sonnet 3), *unbuild* (*Coriolanus*, III. i) and *unfair*, used Sonnet 5 to mean 'remove the fairness (beauty) of'.

10. WATCHDOG

Watchdog was first recorded in Shakespeare's *The Tempest* (I. ii): 'Hark, hark ... The watch-dogs bark'. A straightforward compound of *watch* and *dog*, the word is one of a number of compounds Shakespeare coined for his plays, many of which are still used today: *chimney-top* (*Julius Caesar*, I. i), *birthplace* (*Coriolanus*, IV. iv), *footfall* (*The Tempest*, II. ii), both *upstairs* and *downstairs* (*Henry IV,*

Part 1, II. v), *water-drops* (*Richard II*, IV. i), *shooting star* (*Richard II*, II. iv), *eyeball* (from the poem *Venus and Adonis*), *hunchbacked* (*Richard III*, IV. iv), *fairyland* (*A Midsummer Night's Dream*, II. i) and *puppy-dog* (*King John*, II. i).

IX

TEN WORDS INVENTED BY OTHER WRITERS

In total, the *Oxford English Dictionary* contains some 3,000,000 quotations taken from many thousands of different sources and the works of hundreds of different authors. Shakespeare, the single most-quoted literary figure, is followed by Sir Walter Scott, Geoffrey Chaucer, John Milton, John Dryden and Charles Dickens, but of all of these it is Chaucer who provides the earliest written evidence for the most words with his works offering the first attestations of some 2,000 English terms, from *abated* to *ygrounded* (a Middle English equivalent of *grounded*). Listed here are ten more words whose creation can similarly be credited to an individual author, with entries here ranging from Jonathan Swift in the early eighteenth century (YAHOO) through to Stephen King (PIE-HOLE) and William Gibson (CYBERSPACE) in the 1980s.

1. CHORTLE

A combination of 'chuckle' and 'snort', the word *chortle* was coined by the English writer Lewis Carroll (the pen-name for Charles Dodgson) for his classic 1871 novel *Through the Looking-Glass*. Carroll is widely celebrated for his linguistic inventiveness as a writer and coined a vast number of similar words, which he termed 'portmanteaux', by combining two or more existing terms. Amongst them are *frumious*, from 'fuming' and 'furious';

mimsy, implying both 'miserable' and 'flimsy'; *frabjous*, from 'fabulous' and 'joyous'; *slithy*, presumably based on 'slimy' and 'lithe'; and *galumphing*, 'triumphantly galloping', used in his poem 'Jabberwocky'.

2. CYBERSPACE
A name for the theoretical 'space' in which communication via the internet or similar electronic means is supposed to take place, the term *cyberspace* is credited to the American-born science-fiction writer William Gibson who coined the word for use in his short story 'Burning Chrome' in 1982. The prefix *cyber-*, as found here and in many other modern words making reference to the internet like *cybersquatting, cybercriminal, cybergeek* and *cybercafé*, is derived from *cybernetics*, the science of communication, which in turn takes its name from the Greek for a skilful pilot or steersman, *kubernetikos*.

3. DREAMSCAPE
Used to describe a dreamt or imagined scene or, more literally, the landscape of a dreamt place, the word *dreamscape* is first attested in a 1958 poem, 'The Ghost's Leavetaking', by the American writer Sylvia Plath. One of twentieth-century America's most important female writers, Plath was known for her inventive use of language, creating such unusual terms as *sleep-talk* (for her poem 'Maudlin' in 1956), *wind-ripped* ('Suicide Off Egg Rock', 1959), *sweat-wet* ('Zoo Keeper's Wife', 1961), and *grrr*, which she used as a verb in her short story for children, *The It-Doesn't-Matter Suit* (1959), describing alleycats 'grrring with admiration'.

4. FREELANCE
The earliest recorded use of the word *freelance* in English comes from Sir Walter Scott's classic novel *Ivanhoe*,

written in 1819. Although today used in reference to a journalist or similar person employed on a project-by-project rather than full-time basis, the term originally described a mercenary knight or soldier with no particular allegiance to any specific country or cause, and who instead offered his services in exchange for money. The word was first recorded in reference to someone who works on a *freelance* basis in 1899.

5. KNICKERBOCKER

Familiar as both the name of a type of loose-fitting breeches (*knickerbockers*) and as the name of a dessert of ice cream and other confectionaries (*knickerbocker glory*), on its first appearance in English the word *knickerbocker* was in fact used to refer to someone descended from the original Dutch settlers of New York. In this sense, the word is derived from a pseudonym of the eighteenth- to nineteenth-century American writer Washington Irving, author of the folktales 'The Legend of Sleepy Hollow' and 'Rip Van Winkle', who published his first major work, a popular, satirical *History of New York*, under the alias Diedrich Knickerbocker in 1809.

6. NERD

The word *nerd* is usually credited to the American children's author Dr Seuss, who used it as the name of a peculiar animal in his 1950 book *If I Ran The Zoo*. The poem was accompanied by a picture of a short, squat, grumpy-looking creature with a long face and straggly white hair that appears more cantankerous than nerdy, leading to some debate whether the subsequent use of *nerd* in reference to a bookish or awkward person (first recorded the following year, in the United States' *Newsweek* magazine) is indeed taken from Dr Seuss. If not, *nerd* could alternatively be derived from *nerts* or *nertz*, a 1920s slang term for 'nonsense' or 'madness'; Mortimer Snerd, a dummy used by the popular American ventriloquist Edgar Bergen in the 1940s and 1950s; or even *knurd*, a humorous reversal of the letters of the word 'drunk', implying that nerds on American college campuses tended to avoid drinking and partying.

7. PIE-HOLE

The earliest recorded meaning of the word *pie-hole* in English is as another word for an eyelet, a hole on a garment through which a lace or cord can be threaded, which derives from an old sixteenth-century Scots dialect word, *py*. As a slang term for the mouth, however, *pie-hole* was first recorded in the American horror writer Stephen King's 1983 novel *Christine*. Whether King himself coined the word in this sense is unknown, but either way it is likely that it is modelled on the earlier term *cake-hole*, which dates from the 1940s.

8. ROBOT

The word *robot* was first used in the 1920 play *R.U.R.* ('*Rossum's Universal Robots*') written by the Czech playwright Karel Čapek, which was first translated into English in 1923. Although the invention of the word is generally credited to Čapek himself, he in turn claimed it was the suggestion of his brother, Josef, who presumably based it on one of a number of existing Czech words including *robotnik*, meaning 'slave', and *robota*, meaning 'drudgery' or 'servitude'. Unlike the modern use of the word, Čapek's *robots* were not automated machines but rather artificial 'people', biological entities of skin and bone that are mass-produced in factories. Originally built to work for humans, the robots eventually coordinate a rebellion and take over the world, leading to the extinction of the human race.

9. TINTINNABULATION

Derived from the Latin *tintinnabulum* (used since the sixteenth century as the name of a type of handbell or series of bells used as a musical instrument), the noun *tintinnabulation*, 'ringing of bells', dates from the nineteenth century in English and is believed to have been coined by the American writer Edgar Allan Poe for his 1831 poem 'The Bells' – 'From the time, time, time ... / To the tintinnabulation that so musically wells / From the bells, bells, bells, bells.' The word is one of several for which Poe's works provide the first recorded use, with others including *sentience* (first found in 'The Fall of the House of Usher', 1839), *multicolour* (in the short tale 'The Landscape Garden', 1842) and *normality* (used in his essay *Eureka*, 1848).

10. YAHOO

Coined by Jonathan Swift as the name of a race of brutish men who appear in his 1726 novel *Gulliver's Travels*, within just a few years of the novel's publication the word *yahoo* began to be used more widely in English as a synonym for any similarly loutish, violent or unsophisticated person, and eventually a hooligan or thug. The word is one of a number of Swift's creations that have found their way into the language, as even some of the most bizarre names used in *Gulliver's Travels* have gained broader, figurative meanings in modern English. The opposite adjectives *Brobdingnagian* ('oversized', 'enormous') and *Lilliputian* ('tiny'), for instance, come from the names of the two contrasting lands of Brobdingnag and Lilliput in the novel; *splacknuck*, the name of a wild creature of Brobdingnag, can be used in English as another name for an unusual-looking person or animal; and both *big-endian* and *little-endian* are used allusively in English to refer to the two rivalling parties in some petty dispute, derived from the great argument amongst the Lilliputians as to which end of a soft-boiled egg should rightly be cracked open.

TEN WORDS DERIVED FROM 'HEAD'

The entries in this section are all descended from some root word either meaning or pertaining to the head, with the ten listed here having entered English from as diverse a group of languages as French, Welsh and Afrikaans. Besides such familiar terms as *headlight*, *headcount* and *headline*, the word *head* itself has contributed a similarly diverse collection of words to the language, including *head-brand*, a log positioned at the back of a fireplace; *head-fake*, a sporting term for a movement made with the head in an attempt to deceive an opponent; *head-knee*, part of the extended prow of a ship; and *headborough*, an old-fashioned English word for a local parish official or constable. The word *headhunt*, meanwhile, has been used since the 1960s to refer to the deliberate selection of a candidate for a job, but originally referred to the practice common amongst certain tribes of south-east Asia and the Amazon of hunting and killing members of rival tribes and collecting their heads as trophies.

I. CABBAGE

Cabbage was first recorded in English in the late 1300s as *cabache*, a spelling which hints at its original derivation from an old French word, *caboche* or *caboce*, meaning 'head'. This root is also the origin of the obscure English hunting term *cabbage*, meaning 'remove a deer's head at the antlers', which is just one of a number of the word's less familiar meanings. As well as being the name of a vegetable, a *cabbage* can also be a tailor's offcut, an animal's lair, a fascinator or decorative adornment on a hat, a sweetheart, a fool, money and even, in medical or surgical slang, a coronary artery bypass graft or CABG.

2. CAMOUFLAGE

The word *camouflage* is a descendant of the French verb *camoufler*, meaning 'to veil' or 'disguise', which is in turn derived from an earlier Italian word, *camuffare*, combining *capo*, 'head', and *muffare*, 'to muffle'. *Camouflage* is also likely related to *camouflet*, a French slang term for cigarette smoke blown into a person's face, which gained a military context in English in the mid-nineteenth century when it came to be used to describe the smoking crater or cavern formed by a subterranean bomb. Similarly, on its first appearance in the language (as recently as 1917), *camouflage* was also a military term used to refer to the concealment of ships, guns and other paraphernalia from the enemy. Its zoological sense developed soon afterwards.

3. CAPITULATE

The word *capitulate* has been used as a verb meaning to 'agree' or 'surrender to' since the 1600s, yet on its first appearance in the language almost a century earlier it was originally an adjective, used to describe something set out in a series of directions or chapters; indeed, the verb *capitulate* originally meant 'stipulate' or, literally, to 'draw up under headings'. It is derived from the Latin word *capitulum*, which is itself a derivative of the Latin for 'head', *caput*, from which such familiar English words as *capital, captain, madcap* and both *biceps* and *triceps* ('two-headed' and 'three-headed' muscles, respectively) are all similarly derived.

4. CEPHALOPOD

The prefix *cephalo-* derives from the Ancient Greek word *kephale*, which as well as referring to the most important or topmost part of something was also a Greek word for 'head'. A *cephalopod*, consequently, is a creature with long, leg-like tentacles protruding from its head, like a squid or cuttlefish. The same root is found in a number of other English words, including *encephalitis*, an inflammation of the brain; *cephalomancy*, a form of divination in which the head is physically examined; and *cephalostat*, a type of headrest used during surgical operations. *Bucephalus*, the legendary horse of Alexander the Great, meanwhile, had a name literally meaning 'ox-headed'.

5. CORPORAL

Dating from the early fifteenth century, the adjective *corporal*, meaning 'bodily' or 'physical' (as in *corporal punishment*), is derived from the Latin for 'body', *corpus*, from which a number of other words like *corpse* and *incorporate* are also derived. The military rank of *corporal*, however, dates from the late sixteenth century and is believed to be alternatively derived from its Italian equivalent *caporale*, a derivation of the Italian word for 'head', *capo*, implying that a *corporal* would have been in charge of a body of troops.

6. KOP

First used in English in the 1830s, *kop* is a South African word for a hill derived via Afrikaans from an identical Dutch word meaning 'head'. Only occasionally used in this geographical sense in English, the word is probably most familiar to British English speakers as a nickname used at certain football grounds – and in particular Anfield, home ground of Liverpool FC – for the largest or uppermost of the spectators' terraces. In this context, *kop* has been adopted from Spion Kop, the name of a hill near Ladysmith in the east of South Africa that in January 1900 was the site of a famous battle of the Boer War. Six years later, Anfield's Walton Breck Road stand was nicknamed the 'Spion Kop' by a local journalist who likened the sight of the 25,000 Liverpool supporters it accommodated to the Boer troops that had covered the hill ahead of the battle. The name has since been transferred to several other grounds across England, including those of Leeds United, Sheffield United and Sheffield Wednesday.

7. KOWTOW

Dating from the early nineteenth century, the word *kowtow* is typically used in English as a verb meaning to 'grovel' or 'give in to', or else to 'act in an obsequious manner'. It is of Chinese origin, derived from the Chinese phrase *k'o-t'ou*, literally meaning to 'knock the head', and in its earliest use in English referred to an ancient Chinese custom in which a person would place their forehead on the ground as a mark of deep respect or as an act of submission.

8. PENGUIN

Although its exact origin is debatable, it seems likely that the word *penguin* originally derived from the Welsh phrase *pen gwyn*, literally meaning 'white head'. Quite how a bird living in the furthest reaches of the southern hemisphere came to have a Welsh name, however, is something of a mystery, but it has been suggested that the word was first applied to the great auk, a large, flightless and now extinct black-and-white seabird once native to the North Atlantic. When European explorers first saw penguins on voyages to the southern hemisphere – the word was first recorded in writing in the logbook of Sir Francis Drake's *Golden Hind* in 1577 – it is likely that they simply mistook the birds they saw for the auks they knew back home.

9. POLEAX

The word *poleax* dates from as far back as the fourteenth century in English as the name of a type of short-handled axe, variously used to cut ropes, butcher meat, slaughter animals, and as a close-combat weapon. It is derived from *poll*, an equally old English word for the top of the head, implying that as a weapon the *poleax* would have been especially effective in breaking the heads of animals or adversaries. As a verb, meaning to 'kill', *poleax* dates from the late nineteenth century, whilst the figurative use of the word to mean to 'stun' or 'utterly astonish' developed in the 1950s.

10. TESTY

Used since the early 1500s in English to mean 'irritable' or 'tetchy', on its first appearance in the language the adjective *testy* actually meant 'impetuous' or 'courage-ously headstrong', the sense by which it appears in the works of Geoffrey Chaucer as far back as the 1370s. It is derived from an Old French word for 'head', *teste*, from which the Modern French word *tête* is also derived.

XI

TEN WORDS DERIVED FROM 'HEART'

The Chinese cabbage, the ACCORDION and an old-fashioned English word for a mercy blow may not appear to have all that much in common, yet each one – like all of the entries in this chapter – is descended from some original root word meaning 'heart'. The word *heart* itself is amongst the earliest recorded words in the entire English language, first attested in the text of an Anglo-Saxon psalter written in the early ninth century. As well as being the principal organ of the circulatory system, a *heart* can also be the core or centre of a fruit or vegetable; the central strand of a rope or string around which all others are tied; the sole of a horse's foot; or the driest and innermost part of the trunk of a tree. In the Middle Ages *heart* was even used as an alternative name for the stomach, in the metaphorical sense of it being the source of a person's energy and vigour.

I. ACCORDION

The *accordion* was patented by the Austrian organ-maker Cyrill Demian in 1829, with the first mention to it in written English dating from the following year. Demian took the name of his invention from the much earlier musical term *accord* (essentially meaning 'harmony', as opposed to *discord*), which is in turn descended via French from the Latin *accordare*, meaning 'to reconcile', and ultimately the Latin word for 'heart', *cor*. The word *concord*, meaning 'agreement' or 'unity', is of similar origin.

2. ANACARD

Anacard is a fairly obscure alternative name for the cashew nut or cashew tree. Dating from the mid-sixteenth century in English, it is derived at length from the Ancient Greek words *ana*, roughly meaning 'according to', and *kardia*, meaning 'heart', and is said to refer to the cashew nut's unusual curved shape. *Kardia* is also the origin of a whole host of other English words, including medical terms such as *cardiac*, *cardiograph* and *tachycardia*, an abnormally fast pulse rate.

3. CHOY SUM

The name of a type of Chinese cabbage with soft edible leaves and flowers, *choy sum* is derived from the Cantonese *choi sam*, literally meaning 'vegetable heart'; indeed, the name is sometimes used more generally to refer to the tender inner leaves and stems of other Asian vegetables like bok choy. Similarly, *dim sum*, a Chinese dish typically eaten as a light snack or appetiser, is said to have a name literally meaning 'touch the heart'.

4. CONTRECOEUR

Something said to be done *à contrecoeur* is done reluctantly, or else against one's will or better judgement. First used in English in the early nineteenth century, the term is a direct borrowing from French, where historically it was used in the expression *avoir contrecoeur* to mean 'to have an aversion to' or 'to dislike'. The word is a straightforward compound of the French words *contre*, meaning 'against' (related to the English *counter*, as in *counteract* or *counter-clockwise*), and *coeur*, meaning 'heart'.

5. CORDILOQUY

The English suffix *-loquy* derives from the Latin verb *loquor* meaning 'to speak', and hence is typically found in words conveying some sense of speech or talking, like *soliloquy* (a 'private speech made by a character in a play'), *somniloquy* ('talking in one's sleep') and *obloquy* ('abusive language', derived from the Latin *ob*, meaning 'against'). Similarly, *cordiloquy* is a rarely used English word for a heartfelt speech, derived from *cor*, the Latin word for 'heart', and invented by the seventeenth-century historian Thomas Fuller in his 1642 work *The Holy State and the Profane State*: 'might I coin the word cordiloquie,' he explains, '[for] when men draw the doctrines out of their hearts'.

6. COURAGE

First used in English in the 1300s, the word *courage* originally referred to a person's spirit, or their disposition or temperament. It is derived, via the French *corage*, from the Latin word *cor*, which as well as meaning 'heart' in an anatomical sense could also be used figuratively to mean 'soul' or 'spirit'. *Courage* did not come to mean 'bravery' until the late fourteenth century, but could also be used to mean 'vigour' or 'lustfulness'. In some contexts it was even used to refer to a person's innermost thoughts or intentions, the somewhat obscure sense by which it appears in Shakespeare's *Timon of Athens* (III. iii): 'for my mind's sake; / I'd such a courage to do him good'.

7. FRENZY

Frenzy is one of several English words – including *frenetic*, *frantic* and *phrenology* – derived from the Ancient Greek root *phren* or *phrenos*, generally translated as 'the mind' or 'mental capacity' (as in *schizophrenia*, literally a 'cut mind'). In early Greek, however, *phrenos* could also be used to refer to the heart or the breast, as it was once maintained by some Greek scholars that the basis of a person's mentality lay not in their brain but in their heart, and hence any disorder of the chest could cause mental illness or upset. Dating from the fourteenth century in English, a *frenzy* was originally a 'state of insanity' or 'delirium', with the later and slightly weaker sense of 'excitement' or 'agitation' developing in the early fifteenth century. The idea that the heart is the seat of human emotion and strength, meanwhile, is maintained in words like *lionhearted, open-hearted* and *broken-hearted.*

8. MACHREE

Dating from the seventeenth century, *machree* is one of several Irish terms of endearment to have made their way into the English language. A corruption of the Irish *mo chroí*, literally meaning 'my heart', the use of *machree* in English was popularized in the early 1900s by *Mother Machree*, the title of a popular folksong and novel adapted for cinema by John Ford in 1928. Other similar terms of endearment include *macushla*, derived from the Irish *mo chuisle*, meaning 'my pulse' or 'heartbeat', and *acushla*, a contraction of *a chuisle mo chroí*, literally 'the pulse of my heart'.

9. MISERICORD

The word *misericord* is derived via French from the Latin *misericordia*, meaning 'mercy' or 'pity', which is in turn formed from the Latin *miser*, meaning 'wretched', and *cor*, meaning 'heart'. First recorded in the thirteenth century in a famous Christian monastic manual known as the *Ancrene Riwle*, at its earliest the word was used to mean simply 'compassion' or 'pity', but over the centuries it developed several other meanings and uses, including a 'small blade or dagger, specifically one used to finish off a dying opponent' (fourteenth century); a 'projecting ledge on the underside of a church seat, used to support a person when standing' (early sixteenth century); and a 'room in a monastery or convent in which the rules adhered to by the resident monks or nuns could be relaxed' (mid-sixteenth century).

10. PERQUEER

An obscure and somewhat old-fashioned word almost entirely exclusive to Scottish English, *perqueer* dates from the late fifteenth century. It is derived from an Old French phrase, *par cour*, literally meaning 'by heart', and indeed on its first appearance in the language *perqueer* meant 'known from memory' or 'word for word'. Over time, however, the word came to imply a number of other meanings including 'skilfully made', 'knowledgeable', 'without question' and 'distinct' or 'clearly visible'. It has long since slipped out of widespread use and today survives in only a handful of local Scottish dialects.

XII

TEN WORDS DERIVED FROM 'HAND'

Statistically, *hand* is one of the most fruitful words in the entire English language. It is the most frequently mentioned part of the body and the tenth most frequently used noun in all written English (more common even than words like *woman, place* and *work*), and is recorded in more than 400 different senses and expressions in the *Oxford English Dictionary*. To do something at the *best hand*, for instance, is to do so at the most affordable rate; to have *long hands* means to have great power or influence; to be *hand-and-glove* with someone means to be very closely associated or related; and to do something *hand over head* means to act recklessly or indiscriminately, without considering the consequences. Perhaps one of the most unusual *hand* words, however, is the eighteenth-century term *hand of glory*, a translation of the French *main de gloire* used to refer to a lucky charm or talisman made from the severed and dried hand of an executed criminal.

I. ABDEST
In Islam, *abdest* is the ritual washing of the body before handling the Qur'an, as opposed to other washing rituals like *wudu* and *ghusl* (the partial and entire cleansing of the body respectively) and *tayammum* (a type of dry ablution using sand or dust). *Abdest* was first recorded in English in the seventeenth century and is derived via

62

Turkish from the Persian words *ab*, meaning 'water', and *dest*, meaning 'hand' or 'forearm'.

2. AMANUENSIS
Amanuensis is a Latin loanword originating in Ancient Rome, where it specifically referred to a slave acting as secretary or scribe to an official figure – the term itself is descended from the Latin *servus a manu*, literally meaning 'servant at hand'. In English, *amanuensis* first appeared in the early seventeenth century, when it was used for someone employed to take dictation or copy manuscripts, before gaining a broader sense of an office clerk or secretary in the 1800s.

3. BAISEMAIN
The French word *baisemain* is the proper name for a kiss on the hand used as a greeting or a sign of courtesy, whilst in its plural form the word can be used to mean 'respects' or 'compliments'. Dating from the late sixteenth century in English, the term is derived directly from the French words *baise*, meaning 'kiss', and *main*, meaning 'hand', and historically was used as a sign of feudal submission or homage between a vassal and a lord.

4. CHIROPODIST
Despite the fact that it now refers to a medical professional dealing purely with the feet, when it was first coined in the late 1700s the word *chiropodist* applied to someone able to treat diseases of both the feet and hands; it is derived from the Greek roots *chiro-* and *pod-*, meaning 'hand' and 'foot' respectively. The adjective *chiropractic*, referring to medical treatment involving the manipulation of the spine, is of similar origin, combined with the Greek word *praktikos*, meaning 'practical'.

5. COMMANDO

The word *commando* first entered the English language via Afrikaans during the South African Frontier Wars of the late 1700s, when it originally described an armed and mounted unit of men, typically employed to reclaim stolen property and land. The first use of the word in the modern sense of a specially trained assault troop is credited to Winston Churchill in the 1940s who likely encountered the word during his own military service in South Africa during the Boer War. Predating its appearance in both English and Afrikaans, however, the word was originally a derivative of the Portuguese verb *commandar*, meaning 'to command', which is in turn taken from the Latin *commandare*, literally meaning 'to give into one's hand', or 'to deliver over'. All of these are ultimately derived from the Latin word for 'hand', *manus.*

6. EMANCIPATION

Broadly meaning 'the act of setting free', the first specific use of the word *emancipation* in reference to slavery dates from the early 1700s. Before then, the word was used to refer to an obsolete process from Ancient Roman law through which children were freed from the absolute control of the male head of the family, the *pater familias*, and from the Roman rule of *patria potestas*, a man's legal authority over his family. The word itself is derived from the Latin for 'owner' or 'possessor', *manceps*, which is in turn a combination of the Latin words for 'hand', *manus*, and 'take', *capio.*

7. HANDICAP

The word *handicap* was first used in English in the mid-1600s and is believed to be derived from *hand-in-cap*, the name of an old gambling game used as a method of trading since the fourteenth century. In the game, two traders would each offer up an item for exchange, with a neutral umpire then independently determining any difference in value between the two (known as the 'boot' or 'odds'), which the owner of the less valuable item would be obliged to add to the exchange. Both traders would then place a small amount of money for forfeit into a hat: if they agreed to the umpire's 'odds' they would drop their money into the hat, but if they disagreed, they would keep it in their hand. The trade would only go ahead so long as both parties were in agreement, in which case the umpire would be rewarded for his fairness by keeping the forfeited cash, but if just one or neither party agreed, the umpire would lose out and no trade would take place. *Handicap* continued to be used in this way long into the eighteenth century, when it began to be adopted in horse racing to describe a race in which any inconsistencies in the abilities of the horses would be assessed and superior horses would be laden with excess weights. The word then came to be used for these excess weights themselves in the nineteenth century, and ultimately, in the 1890s, for any encumbrance or disabling factor that makes a task more difficult.

8. HANDSOME

On its first appearance in the language in the early 1400s the word *handsome* literally meant 'easy to handle' or 'close at hand', and as such is derived directly from the English word *hand* and the unusual suffix -*some*, used to indicate a certain quality or characteristic, as in *troublesome*, *awesome* or *flavoursome*. Over time, use of *handsome* developed from 'handy' or 'usable' to mean 'suitable' or 'appropriate' (early 1500s); 'clever', 'graceful' or 'decent' (mid-1500s); 'considerable, ample' (late 1500s); and finally 'seemly', 'polite' or, as it is most used today, 'fine looking', the sense by which it is found in Shakespeare's *Othello* (IV. iii): 'Lodovico is a proper man ... / A very handsome man.'

9. LEGERDEMAIN

Adopted directly into English from French, the word *legerdemain* was first recorded in English as *lygarde-de-mayne* in a work by the prolific English monastic poet John Lydgate in the early fifteenth century. Another word for trickery or sleight of hand, the word is formed simply from the French *léger de main*, literally meaning 'light (that is, not heavy) of hand'. A handful of later derivatives, including *legerdemainish*, meaning 'magical' or 'dexterously', and *legerdemainist*, another name for a conjuror or trickster, appeared in the 1800s but have remained rarely used.

10. MANIFESTO

The word *manifesto* was adopted into English from Italian in the early 1600s. A derivative of the Italian *manifestare*, meaning 'to reveal' or 'to show', the word is ultimately descended from the Latin adjective *manifestus*, meaning 'plainly clear' or 'obvious' (the same root from which the English *manifest* is also derived), which was once used in legal contexts to refer to criminals who were either caught in the act or to that which can be proven guilty without any doubt. The root of all of these forms is the Latin word for 'hand', *manus*.

XIII

TEN WORDS DERIVED FROM 'FOOT'

The word *foot* has been recorded as far back in the English language as the early ninth century, from where it has since developed dozens of different meanings and senses and can now be used as a noun, a verb and, much less frequently, as an adjective meaning 'lowly' or 'mundane'. As the name of a unit of measurement, *foot* dates from the eleventh century and was so named as it roughly corresponded to the length of a man's foot. The first reference to the *foot of a bed* dates from the early fourteenth century and to the *foot of a page* from the mid-1600s, whilst *football* was first mentioned in English in the Football Act of 1424, passed by King James I of Scotland, which banned the game and made playing it punishable by a fine of four pence. Although the act eventually fell out of use, it officially remained in operation until it was finally repealed in 1906.

1. EXPEDITE
Meaning to 'advance' or 'accelerate the progress of', particularly by removing obstacles or other difficulties, the word *expedite* dates from the early seventeenth century in English, and is derived directly from the Latin verb *expedire*, which variously meant 'to set right', or 'to procure or obtain'. In turn, this original Latin form comprises the prefix *ex-*, meaning 'out' or 'from', and the Latin word for 'foot', *pes* or *pedis*, and so literally means to 'unfetter

the feet', and hence to 'free from restraints'. The opposite word, incidentally, was the Latin verb *impedire*, from which English has since derived the word *impede*.

2. OCTOPUS

It is a misconception that the word *octopus* means either 'eight-legged' or 'eight-armed', as in fact the suffix *-pus* is derived from the Ancient Greek word for 'foot', *pous*, meaning that the *octopus* is actually an 'eight-footed' creature. The *platypus*, meanwhile, is a 'flat-footed' creature and takes the first part of its name from the Greek *platys*, meaning 'flat' or 'broad'. It is also a misconception that the correct plural of words like *octopus* and *platypus* should be *octopi* and *platypi*, as this would only be true if they were of Latin origin – as Greek names their correct plural forms should in fact be *octopodes* and *platypodes*.

3. OPPIDUM

In archaeology, an *oppidum* is a large and often heavily defended Iron Age settlement, of a type that emerged across Western Europe in the second and first centuries BC. Typically, *oppida* were positioned on areas of high flat ground, were often walled or fortified for protection and served as the largest settlement or stronghold for much of the surrounding area. The word itself first appeared in English in late nineteenth century, but it was originally a Roman name for any similarly defended town or castle. Indeed, it is often claimed that Julius Caesar was the first to apply the name *oppidum* to the fortified settlements he encountered across Europe during his conquest of Gaul in the first century BC, which still bear the name today. Although the origin of the word is unclear, it seems likely that it is in some way related to the Latin word for 'foot', *pes*, perhaps via some earlier word meaning 'footprint', in the sense of a flattened and enclosed area of land.

4. PEDIGREE

The word *pedigree* dates from the mid-fifteenth century in English when it originally referred to a family tree or similar genealogical diagram drawn to depict the lineage of a person or dynasty. It was not until the mid-1800s that it came to be used as an adjective describing a pure-bred creature, and it was as recently as the 1950s that this adjective came again to be used as a noun as another name for a thoroughbred animal with documented ancestry. The word *pedigree* itself is of French origin, and is formed from a contraction of the Anglo-Norman phrase *pé de grue*, literally meaning 'stork's foot', as the narrow, elongated claws of the stork were said to resemble the thin lines drawn on a family tree to connect relatives and generations to one another.

5. PESSIMISM

In English, the word *pessimism* was first used in the late eighteenth century to describe a state of absolute decay, or else something of the worst possible quality or condition. It was not until the mid-nineteenth century that this meaning was adapted to refer to a gloomy, negative worldview or to a tendency to focus on the worst aspect of any given thing. The word itself is derived from the Latin adjective *pessimus*, meaning 'worst' or 'bottommost' – *pessimum*, the rarely used opposite of the more familiar *optimum*, is of similar origin. *Pessimus* is in turn believed to be a derivative of the same ancient root as the Latin word for 'foot', *pes*, in the sense that the feet are the lowest or bottommost part of the body.

6. PIEDMONT

Piedmont is a compound of the Italian words for 'foot', *piede*, and 'mountain', *monte*. It is probably most familiar to English speakers as a place name notably borne by the Piedmont region of north-eastern Italy located, appropriately enough, at the foot of the Swiss Alps. In more general use, however, the word has been applied since the mid-nineteenth century to any expanse of land situated at the foot of a mountain or mountain range, and in North America is often used to refer to the vast fertile plateau located on the eastern side of the Appalachian Mountains, which stretches from New Jersey to Alabama.

7. PODIUM

The word *podium* is derived at length from the Greek word for the base of a vase, *podion*, which is itself based on the Greek for 'foot', *pous*. In English, the term dates back to the late seventeenth century when it was originally used in architectural contexts to refer to a kind of raised platform encircling a Roman arena, and it was not until the late eighteenth century that it came to be used for a base or plinth upon which something is stood. The more modern use of *podium* as another name for a raised dais or lectern at the front of an auditorium dates from 1899, while the first reference to a *winner's podium* was recorded in an American newspaper in 1948.

8. POLYP

Dating from the early 1400s in English, the word *polyp* was first used to refer to a tumour or lump located specifically in the nasal passages, before later being used for any similar growth found elsewhere in the body. It is a shortening of the Latin equivalent term *polypus*, which as well as being used for a bodily growth was oddly also the name of a type of octopus or cuttlefish: the word literally means 'many-footed' and is ultimately derived from the Ancient Greek prefix *poly-*, meaning 'many' or 'more than one', and *pous*, meaning 'foot'.

9. SESQUIPEDALIAN

The adjective *sesquipedalian* appropriately means 'pertaining to or given to using long words'. It dates from the early seventeenth century in English, and is a Latin loanword adopted directly into the language from a famous quotation from *Ars Poetica* (*The Art of Poetry*), a first-century BC essay by the Roman poet Horace in which he derides the use of extremely long words, or what he terms '*sesquipedalia verba*'. The word *sesquipedalian* itself is formed from the Latin prefix *sesqui-*, typically used in reference to quantities and measurements to mean 'half as much again' or 'one-and-a-half times', and the Latin word *pes*, meaning 'foot' – the term literally refers to words that are 'a foot and a half' in length.

10. SUPPLANT

Meaning to 'replace' or 'usurp', the verb *supplant* dates from the fourteenth century, when it was used more specifically to refer to a dispossession or overthrow, particularly one made through violent or dishonourable means. It is derived from the Latin verb *supplantare*, meaning literally 'to trip' or 'to stumble', which is itself formed from a compound of *sub*, meaning 'under', and *planta*, 'the sole of the foot'. Of similar origin is the zoological term *plantigrade*, used to describe creatures like bears, mice, rabbits and humans that walk on the soles of their feet.

XIV

TEN WORDS DERIVED FROM 'LIGHT'

The ten entries listed in this chapter are all derived from some root word meaning 'light', in the sense of brightness or lustre. Found as *leoht* in Old English, *light* itself has more than 200 different derivations in the *Oxford English Dictionary*, and is the source of a great many more idiomatic phrases and expressions. To *see the light*, for instance, meaning to 'understand' or 'realize', dates from the seventeenth century; to see something in a *good* or *bad light* is a sixteenth-century expression, as is to *stand in someone's light*, meaning to rob someone of their enjoyment of something; whilst to *come to light*, meaning to 'emerge' or be 'revealed', is almost as old as the word *light* itself, and is recorded in an Old English text dating from the tenth century.

I. ANTELUCAN
The adjective *antelucan* relates to the hours immediately before dawn, and is typically used in relation to religious practices or services. Dating from the mid-seventeenth century in English, the word is derived directly from its Latin equivalent *antelucanus*, which is formed from a compound of the preposition *ante*, meaning 'before' or 'in front of' (as in *antemeridian* and *antechamber*), and *lux*, the Latin word for 'light'.

2. APHENGESCOPE

Developed in the eighteenth century, an *aphengescope* is a 'magic lantern', a type of projector uniquely capable of producing enlarged images of solid objects, rather than simply shining a light through a transparency. First mentioned in English in the 1860s, like other lanterns of this type the *aphengescope* worked by shining a light or series of lights on to a non-transparent object, with a complex series of mirrors and lenses used to project and focus a larger image of the object on to a nearby screen. The word itself is coined from a series of Greek roots, principally the prefix *a-*, denoting an absence or lack of something, and *phengos*, meaning 'light' or 'lustre'.

3. ÉCLAIR

The word *éclair* was first recorded in English in an article in New York's *Vanity Fair* magazine as early as 1861. A derivative of the French verb *éclairer*, meaning 'to shed light on' or 'to brighten' – which is in turn taken from the Latin verb *exclarare*, meaning 'to light up' or 'to make clear' – *éclair* is actually the French word for a flash of lightning, although quite how this name came to be applied to a choux pastry finger is something of a mystery.

4. FANTASY

Fantasy first appeared in English in the early fourteenth century, when it was originally used to refer to a mental image of an object or to the mental capacity by which such an image is formed. Over time, the word developed a number of other meanings and senses including a hallucination or apparition (1300s), a desire (late 1300s), a speculation (mid-1400s), imagination (1500s) and, more recently, a daydream exploring a person's desires

(1920s), and a literary genre featuring imaginary and otherworldly characters and creatures (1940s). The word itself is thought to have entered English from French yet originally derives from the Latin *phantasia*, meaning 'imagination' or 'apparition', and in turn the Greek *phantos*, meaning 'to show in light' or 'to make visible', which is itself a derivation of the Ancient Greek word for 'light', *phos*.

5. ILLUSTRATION

The word *illustration* – along with a handful of similar terms like *lustre* and *illustrious* – is derived from the Latin verb *lucere*, meaning 'to shine', and ultimately *lux*, the Latin word for 'light'. On its first appearance in the language in the mid-fifteenth century, *illustration* meant 'enlightenment' or 'illumination', specifically of the mind or spirit, before its meaning developed to come to refer to any clarifying or elucidating factor (1500s), then to the act of making something distinctive (1600s), and lastly, in the early 1800s, to a pictorial embellishment used to explain or enhance a text.

6. KOH-I-NOOR

The Koh-i-noor is a magnificent 186-carat, 37 g diamond unearthed in the Andhra Pradesh region of eastern India sometime before the sixteenth century. First mentioned in English in the 1700s, in India the Koh-i-noor has been traced back to texts dating from the mid-1500s and is believed to have a name meaning 'mountain of light' in Ancient Persian. The diamond has been held in the Crown Jewels of the United Kingdom from the reign of Queen Victoria onwards. In the years since it was first brought to Britain in the nineteenth century the word *koh-i-noor* has gained both a general meaning in English referring to any similarly large or garish stone, and a figurative meaning referring to anything considered the best or most superb of its kind.

7. LUCUBRATE

Dating from the seventeenth century, the verb *lucubrate* is today generally taken to mean to 'write in a scholarly manner', implying that the writer has carried out a great deal of laborious research or else has gone into an unnecessarily elaborate amount of detail; a *lucubration* is another word for an extensive and well-informed written work. The earliest and most literal meaning of the word, however, is to 'work by artificial light', with the implication that the *lucubrator* would work long into the night on their studies. The word is derived from its Latin equivalent *lucubrare*, which is ultimately descended from the Latin word for 'light', *lux*.

8. LYNX

Eurasian lynx were native to Great Britain until they were hunted to extinction in the Middle Ages. Nevertheless, the creatures were widely known in the Middle English period and are recorded in the language as early as the mid-fourteenth century. The word *lynx* itself was adopted into the language via Latin, and is ultimately descended from the creature's Ancient Greek name *lunx*, which is in turn believed to be a form of the Greek *leukos*, meaning 'white' or 'light', presumably referring to the cat's distinctively reflective eyes.

9. PHOSPHORUS

The discovery of *phosphorus* (P), chemical element number 15, in the mid-seventeenth century is credited to the German alchemist Hennig Brand, who produced a glow-in-the-dark phosphate compound, ammonium sodium hydrogen phosphate, by boiling and distilling his own urine in his Hamburg laboratory in 1669; *phosphorus* was the first chemical element discovered in modern times. Brand called the light-emitting substance he discovered *phosphorus mirabilis*, the 'miraculous bearer of light', deriving its name from the Greek words for 'light', *phos*, and 'to bring' or 'to carry', *phero*. In English, however, the first recorded use of the word *phosphorus* was not in reference to the element but rather as a proper noun, *Phosphorus*, which was used as an alternative name for the Morning Star by astronomers in the late sixteenth century.

10. RADIUS

The word *radius* has a variety of different meanings and usages in English, the earliest of which is as the name of the shorter of the two bones of the human forearm, first described in English in the mid-1500s. Amongst the word's many other meanings, however, are the fin of a fish or ray; the arm of a starfish; a device used to measure the altitude of the sun or a star; the upright post or shaft of a wooden cross; the area within which something operates; a line joining the centre of a circle to the circumference; and, similarly, the spoke of a wheel. The word itself comes from the identical Latin word *radius*, which, amongst a similarly large group of meanings, could also be used to refer to a ray of light.

XV

TEN WORDS DERIVED FROM 'BIRD'

The Latin word for 'bird', *avis*, is itself found in English in the unusual seventeenth-century expression *rara avis*, literally meaning a 'rare bird', which is used to describe anything or anyone rarely seen or encountered, or else that providing an exceptional or unusual example of its type. As well as being the root of AUSPICES, AVIATION and OCARINA, *avis* is also the origin of a handful of much less familiar English words including *aviculture*, the rearing or breeding of birds; *pulveratrix*, an ornithological term for any bird that cleans its feathers by bathing in dust or sand; and *aucupate*, an old verb literally meaning to 'go bird-catching', but now used figuratively to mean to 'hunt' or 'chase'. The name of the scientific study of birds, *ornithology*, is alternatively derived from the Ancient Greek word for 'bird', *ornis* (as is ORNOMANCY, below), yet on its first appearance in English in the mid-seventeenth century was used to describe an essay or written description of bird songs.

1. AUSPICES

Used in English since the sixteenth century, in Ancient Rome *auspices* were signs and omens interpreted by Roman augurs as messages from the gods. Although many natural phenomena were seen as prophetic to the official diviners of Rome, the *auspex* (of which *auspices* is the plural) was a diviner specifically skilled in the interpretation of birds, the term itself being derived from the Latin for 'bird', *avis*, and 'observer' or 'watcher', *spex*. Omens like these were held in great regard in Roman society – the legendary founders of Rome, Romulus and Remus, are said to have decided on the city's location based on their observation of vultures. Ultimately many important legal and political affairs would be withheld until the opinion of the gods had been considered; important figures were not *inaugurated* into office until the augur's divinations had been interpreted.

2. AVIATION

Defined as 'the science of powered flight', the word *aviation* was borrowed into English from French in the mid-nineteenth century, from where it is derived from the Latin word for 'bird', *avis*. The first recorded use of the term in English dates from 1866 when it appeared in a translation of a work, *Right to Fly*, by the noted French writer and artist Gaspard-Félix Tournachon, better known by the pseudonym 'Nadar'. As well as being a noted journalist, caricaturist and photographer, Nadar was also obsessed with the concept of heavier-than-air flight and was a keen amateur balloonist – in fact, he is credited with having taken the first known aerial photographs from a balloon of his own design and construction in the mid-1850s.

3. LADYBIRD

The word *ladybird* dates in English from the sixteenth century, and was first recorded in Shakespeare's *Romeo and Juliet* (III. iii) in 1597. At its very earliest the word was actually used as a term of endearment for a young woman, and it was not until the late seventeenth century that it began to be used as a name for the colourful beetles that bear the name today. Although the precise origin of the word is questionable, *lady* is popularly said to refer to the Virgin Mary, with the insect's spots said to represent the Seven Sorrows of Mary in Christian tradition, while *bird* has been used in English as an epithet for a young woman or girl since the fifteenth century – its later association with an insect is probably just a reference to its ability to fly.

4. NEOSSOLOGY

Neossology is the specific branch of ornithology that deals with the incubation of eggs and the rearing of hatchlings. Albeit a fairly obscure and rarely used term, the word was coined by the renowned British zoologist and ornithologist Alfred Newton, an early proponent of evolution by natural selection, in 1865. It is derived from the Greek *neossos*, meaning 'young bird', whilst the similar term *neossoptiles* is the proper name for the soft, downy feathers of a young bird.

5. OCARINA

An *ocarina* is a musical instrument consisting of a hollow, egg-shaped body with several finger holes and a separate mouthpiece protruding from the side. One of the simplest and oldest of all wind instruments, with similar forms dating back several thousand years, the development of the modern *ocarina* – which has a greater range of notes and a stronger sound than its ancient ancestors – is credited to the nineteenth- to twentieth-century Italian inventor Giuseppe Donati. Its name is the Italian for 'little goose', said to be a reference to its unusual shape: the Italian word for 'goose', *oca*, is derived from its Latin equivalent, *auca*, which is in turn a diminutive of the Latin for 'bird', *avis*.

6. ORNOMANCY

Dating from the early 1500s, the word *ornomancy* is the earliest of several English words – including *ornithomancy* (mid-1600s), *orneoscopis* (mid-1700s) and *orniscopy* (late 1800s) – that refer to divination made through the observation of birds. The root of all of these terms, and many more like them, is the Greek word for 'bird', *ornis*, which is itself used in English to describe the collective bird species native to a specific area, much in the same way that the Latin *flora* and *fauna* are used to refer to an area's plant and animal life. Of similar derivation are such unusual words as *ornithopter*, a machine designed to fly using artificial flapping wings; *ornithoid*, an adjective describing anything pertaining to or resembling a bird or a bird's egg; and *ornithocoprophilous*, a zoological adjective describing anything that grows on bird droppings.

7. SIMURGH

The *simurgh* is a gigantic mythological bird of prey from Asian legend, whose name has also been used allusively in English since the late nineteenth century to refer to any gigantic flying creature or object. Known throughout Middle Eastern legend but most particularly associated with Iran, the word *simurgh* is derived from the Persian words for 'eagle', *sin*, and 'bird', *murgh*. The creature is typically depicted as female, with the face and body of a dog or lion, and appears in a vast number of Iranian and Kurdish folktales wherein it is often portrayed as a pure, peaceful and supremely wise creature said to have amassed an unparalleled knowledge of the world over its vast lifespan.

8. TORII

Tori is the Japanese word for 'bird', familiar to English-speakers as part of the names of popular Japanese dishes like *yakitori*, grilled skewered chicken. The derivative *torii*, which literally means 'bird-perch', is a Japanese word for the traditional entrance to a Shinto shrine, typically marked by a grand monument comprising two upright posts (known as *hashira*) joined by two horizontal posts, one slightly lower than the other (the *nuki*), with the uppermost of the two (the *kasagi*) usually curved slightly upwards and projecting from the sides.

9. WANDERVOGEL

Wandervogel literally means 'wandering bird' in German, and was originally the name of a late nineteenth- and early twentieth-century youth organization. Originating in a student-led study group founded in Berlin in 1895, over time this initial assembly developed into a wider cultural movement for young German boys, emphasizing outdoor pursuits and an interest in German folk traditions over the increasing materialism of modern city life. Officially founded in 1901, the organization quickly became German's preeminent youth organization of the early twentieth century and the term *wandervogel* soon slipped into common usage as another term for a skilled outdoorsman, or a keen hiker or rambler.

10. WAZOO

Used in a handful of different and equally colourful phrases – like *out of the wazoo*, meaning 'in excess' or 'in abundance', and *the grand wazoo*, referring an important character or bigwig – the slang term *wazoo* was first recorded in English in the 1960s. Aside from the fact that it appears to have originated in North America, the precise origin of the term is a mystery, although it has been suggested that it is probably a development of the French word for 'bird', *oiseau*, originating amongst the Creole languages of the southern United States.

XVI

TEN WORDS DERIVED FROM 'MOTHER'

Remarkably, in almost every language on earth the word for *mother* tends to contain the sound 'm'. As well as all of the familiar English forms like *mum, ma, mom* and *mama*, the *m* trend continues into languages as diverse as Welsh (*mam*), Icelandic (*móðir*), Latin (*mater*), Hebrew (*em*), Vietnamese (*me*), Navajo (*ama*) and even Ancient Egyptian (*mwt*). This association is by no means a random one, however, as the 'm' sound is one of the easiest of all sounds to produce and thus one of the earliest to develop in the first vocalisations of babies, which would under-standably become attached to its closest parent very early in its infancy.

1. ALTRICIAL

The zoological adjective *altricial* describes young creatures – and in particular birds – that are completely helpless after birth and remain confined to their nest, reliant on their parents' care, until they have developed enough to leave. Dating from the mid-nineteenth century, the word is derived from the Latin word for 'foster-mother' or 'wet nurse', *altrix*, which is in turn the feminine form of the Latin word for 'keeper' or 'feeder', *altor*. The root of all of these terms is the verb *alere*, meaning 'to nourish', from which several other English words – including *alimony, alumnus* and *alimentary*, as in *alimentary canal*, another name for the digestive tract – are all similarly derived.

82

2. BELDAM

Dating from as far back as the fifteenth century, in its earliest appearance in English the word *beldam* was used to mean 'grandmother', but in later use was applied more generally to any aged female relative or woman, or else was used depreciatively of an old hag or witch; the derivative *beldamship*, essentially meaning 'grandmother-hood', dates from the mid-1600s. The word *beldam* itself is formed from two long-obsolete English terms: *bel*, an old prefix historically used to denote some kind of relationship or kinship, and *dame*, a Middle English word for 'mother'.

3. CUMMER

Cummer is an old fourteenth-century English name for a godmother, although over time it has also come to be used to describe a gossip or confidante, or else as a general term of address for a young woman. It is one of a number of comparable English words, including *commother*, *kimmer* and *comered*, all of which are related to the equivalent Latin term *commater*, formed from the prefix *com-*, meaning 'together' or 'with', and *mater*, meaning 'mother'.

4. GENETRIX

Genetrix is a Latin word essentially meaning 'mother', often with the implication of a 'creator' or 'ancestor', and as such is descended from the same root – *gignere*, a Latin verb meaning 'to give birth' – as words like *generate*, *genesis*, *ingénue* and *progeny*. In English, *genetrix* was first used in the mid-1500s as a more formal name for a person's mother, but over time this meaning has broadened and today it is also figuratively used to refer to a person's native country or background.

5. MAMMAL

The word *mammal* is a surprisingly recent addition to the English language, recorded no earlier than 1813. It is derived from the Latin taxonomic term *Mammalia*, coined in 1758 by the Swedish zoologist Carl Linnaeus for use in his monumental work *Systema Naturae*, which established the so-called Linnaean system still used today to classify all living things. Linnaeus took his term *Mammalia* from the Latin word for 'breast', *mamma* (as found in similar words such as *mammary* and *mammogram*), and used it to classify all vertebrate creatures that produce milk to suckle their young. In Latin, *mamma* was also used as a child's informal term for its mother, and is ultimately another example of the ancient and instinctive association of the *m* sound to refer to the female parent.

6. MAMMOTHREPT

First recorded in English in Ben Jonson's 1601 play *Cynthia's Revels*, a *mammothrept* is a spoilt child or, by extension, someone with poor judgement or knowledge due to their immaturity or inexperience. Whether or not the word was coined by Jonson himself is unclear, but either way the term has seemingly been adopted from the Ancient Greek *mammothreptos*, a compound of the Greek *mamme*, meaning 'mother', and *trephein*, meaning 'to bring up' or 'to nourish', which was used to refer to a child brought up by its grandmother.

7. MARRAINE

Originating during the First World War, *marraines* – or the *marraines de guerre* – were French women who effectively acted as pen pals to troops serving on the front line in German-occupied France. The *marraine de guerre* scheme was established in 1915 and was quickly taken up by the

French press who encouraged women to 'adopt' a soldier, principally by sending him encouraging letters and parcels of food and other gifts, as an act of patriotism and to help maintain morale amongst troops with no means of contacting their own families. The word *marraine* itself literally means 'godmother' in French and is ultimately a derivation of the Latin *mater*.

8. MATRIX

The word *matrix* has a vast number of different meanings and uses in English, most of which tend to carry some sense of connectivity or supportiveness. As well as an interconnected system or network of individual elements, a *matrix* can be the rock in which a fossil or gemstone is buried; an original sound recording from which copies are made; the bed of a finger or toenail, from where the new nail grows; a clause which contains a subordinate clause; a mould from which something is cast; or the recess into which a metal effigy or trophy is mounted. The earliest of all of the word's meanings, however, dates from as far back as the early 1400s in English, when *matrix* was used as another name for the womb of an animal. In this context, it derived from an Old French term for a pregnant animal, *matris*, which is in turn a derivative of the Latin *mater*, meaning 'mother'.

9. MATTER

The word *matter* was first recorded in English as early as the thirteenth century. It was adopted into the language via French from the earlier Latin word *materia*, which could variously be used to refer to the material from which something is made, to timber or other building materials, or to the innermost and strongest wood of a tree. The root of all of these words is the Latin *mater*, meaning 'mother', which in this sense is used figuratively to refer to the supportive source from which something is made or developed.

10. METROPOLIS

The word *metropolis* literally means 'mother city' and is derived from the two Greek words, *meter* and *polis*, the latter of which was originally used to describe a city-state in Ancient Greece. Despite these origins – and the word's most familiar use today for any large sprawling city – the word's earliest recorded use in English was as an ecclesiastical term describing the see of a so-called *metropolitan* bishop, a high-ranking official in the Christian Church who presided over all of the other bishops of the surrounding province from a central seat.

XVII

TEN WORDS DERIVED FROM 'FATHER'

Father is the modern development of the Old English word *fæder*, which has been recorded in written texts dating from as far back as the ninth century. As well as being used to refer to the male parent, in Old English *fæder* could also be used more generally to refer to any male ancestor or to anyone providing paternal care or advice, or even to anyone in a superior position to oneself.

The ten words listed here are all derived from some original root word meaning 'father', yet the word *father* itself has provided the language with a vast number of derivatives and expressions. Besides familiar terms like *father figure* and *fatherhood*, English has *father-brother*, an old sixteenth-century Scots term for an uncle; *father-better*, an odd seventeenth-century adjective literally meaning 'better than one's father'; and *father-dust*, an eighteenth-century poetic name for pollen. The first recorded reference to *Father Christmas*, meanwhile, dates from the mid-1600s in English, whilst *Father Time* was first mentioned in the mid-1500s.

I. ABBOT
Meaning 'the leader or superior of a group of Christian monks', the word *abbot* – from which the related terms *abbey*, *abbess* and *abbacy* all derive – is the modern development of the Old English word *abbat* or *abbod*, which is itself derived via Latin from the Ancient Greek *abba*, used

as a title of respect for the head of a monastery but literally meaning 'father'. Ultimately, the word is related to the earlier and identical Aramaic word for 'father', *abba*, which is popularly used in Christian scriptures as a means of addressing God.

2. ABELMOSK

First used in English in the early eighteenth century, *abelmosk* is the general name for a small group of tropical plants of the genus *Abelmoschus*, native to central Africa, Asia and northern Australia. The genus includes okra, popularly known as 'lady's fingers' and often used in cookery, and the musk mallow, a yellow-flowering plant of India whose oil was formerly used as a replacement for animal musk in the manufacture of perfume. Indeed, the name *abelmosk* is derived via Italian and Latin from the plant's Arabic name, *abul'misk*, which literally means 'father of the musk'.

3. COMPATRIOT

Meaning 'fellow countryman' or 'neighbour', but often used more loosely to refer to a companion or colleague, the word *compatriot* was first recorded in English in the early seventeenth century. Adopted into the language from its French equivalent *compatriote*, the word is ultimately of Latin origin, formed from the prefix *com-*, meaning 'with', and *patria*, meaning 'homeland' or literally 'fatherland'; *patria* is a form of the Latin adjective *patrius*, meaning 'fatherly'.

4. COMPÈRE

Used since the 1910s as a title for the host of a ceremony or performance, the word *compère* in fact dates back to the early 1700s when it was originally used as another name for a male acquaintance or friend. In its native French, however, *compère* dates back as far as the thirteenth century, when it was used both as a familiar greeting for a male friend (from where the English use of the word appears to have evolved) and as a term roughly equivalent to the English 'godfather', used to refer either to a child's unrelated guardian or to the father of one's own godchild. In this more specific sense, the word is a literal translation of the Latin *compater*, meaning 'with the father'.

5. EDUCATOR

Unlike its modern English equivalent *educate*, the Latin verb *educare* originally meant 'to rear' or 'to raise', especially in the sense of raising livestock or other animals, and as such is based on the earlier Latin verb *ducere* (the source of the English word *duct*), which meant 'to lead' or 'to guide'. The noun *educator*, ultimately, meant 'foster-father' in Latin, and it was not until much later that it came to be used to describe a tutor or teacher, in the sense of someone who helps to raise or guide children. In English, *educator* dates from the early sixteenth century when it too originally meant 'person who rears offspring', and it was not until the seventeenth century that the modern sense of the word began to appear.

6. JUPITER

In Roman mythology, *Jupiter* was the most important of all of the gods, the equivalent of the Greek god Zeus, who was first mentioned in English texts in the early thirteenth century. The name *Jupiter* is actually a contraction of the Latin epithet *Jovis pater*, literally meaning 'Jove father' – *Jove* was *Jupiter*'s earliest name in Latin, which is still retained in some poetic and literary contexts today.

In English, both names have a number of derivatives and are used in various phrases and expressions, including the old-fashioned interjections *by Jove!* or *by Jupiter!* – both of which come from the practice of swearing oaths to the gods in Roman courtrooms. *Jupiter* was also once used as another name for tin, and appears in the names of a number of flowers and plants including *Jupiter's eye* (houseleek, *Sempervivum tectorum*) and *Jupiter's beard* (red valerian, *Centranthus ruber*), whilst *Jove* is the origin of the adjective *jovial*, meaning 'cheerful' or 'good-humoured'.

7. PATERNOSTER

Paternoster literally translates from Latin into English as 'our father', and has been used in Christian tradition as an alternative name for 'The Lord's Prayer' since the early Old English period. As one of the prayers recited during a full Christian rosary, however, in the thirteenth century the name *paternoster* came to be used as an alternative term for a string of rosary beads itself, and since then has gained a considerable number of allusive meanings in English, most of which carry some sense of a chain or series of interconnected objects. The word *paternoster* can be applied to a fishing line with hooks set along it at different intervals (late 1600s); a decorative architectural row of spherical objects or moulds (early 1700s); a method of raising water from a well using a chain of buckets (late 1800s); a type of lift comprising a chain of open-fronted compartments allowing entry and exit at every floor (early 1900s); and a glacial lake forming part of a series of similar lakes linked by a single stream (1940s).

8. PRIMOGENITOR

Specifically used to describe someone's earliest ancestor but often used more broadly in English to refer simply to someone from whom another person is descended, the word *primogenitor* was adopted directly into English from Latin in the mid-seventeenth century. The word is a compound of the Latin adverb *primo*, meaning 'first', and *genitor*, a specific term referring to a male parent – the female equivalent would be a *primogenitrix*.

9. PAPPUS

First described in English in the early eighteenth century, *pappus* is a botanical term for any one of the soft, feathery appendages found on the fruit or seeds of certain plants – like the fluffy white seedheads of flowers such as the dandelion or thistle – which are grown by the plant to aid in their dispersal by the wind. The word is derived directly from Latin, where as well as being used in the same sense as it is in English it was also used to mean 'old man', the white *pappus* hairs said to resemble the white hairs of old age. In this sense, the word is descended from the Ancient Greek word *pappos*, which is a child's word for his father.

10. PATRONIZE

The verb *patronize* dates from the late sixteenth century in English, when it was originally used in a literal sense to mean to 'treat as a patron', or to 'protect' or 'support'. Use of the word became more disparaging over time, however, and by the nineteenth century it was primarily used to refer to a condescending, over-protective or overly friendly manner. The root of the word, *patron*, dates from the early fourteenth century in English and is descended from the Latin *patronus*, meaning 'protector' or 'master', and ultimately the Latin word for 'father', *pater*.

XVIII

TEN WORDS DERIVED FROM 'WORD'

Appropriately, *word* is one of the most commonly used and earliest recorded of all English words, listed amongst the top 3 per cent of those most frequently encountered in the language, and first attested in documents dating from as far back as the ninth century. For such a seemingly straightforward term, historically *word* could be used in quite a complex series of contexts and senses besides simply referring to an individual unit of language; some of these uses are the ancestors of idiomatic expressions still used in English today. A *word* in Old English, for instance, could also be a remark or spoken utterance (a sense retained in the modern phrase *to have a word*); a promise or guarantee (as in *to give one's word*); gossip or news (*to hear word of*); a command or instruction (*to send word*); or a divine proclamation (*the word of God*).

1. APOLOGY

On its first appearance in English in the mid-sixteenth century, the word *apology* initially meant 'plea' or 'defence', or else 'formal justification of something', and was often used in the titles of literary works discussing or supporting a person's actions or beliefs. In this original sense, the word dates back via Latin to the Ancient Greek *apologia*, which referred specifically to a speech made in defence of something – the *Apology of Socrates*, for instance, was a formal explanation of Socrates's charge of 'corrupting the young' and 'not believing in the gods in whom the city believes', famously recounted by his pupil Plato. The word itself is comprised of the Greek *apo*, meaning 'off' or 'from', and *logos*, which in Ancient Greek could variously denote a speech, a thought, a sentence or a word.

2. CRUCIVERBALIST

A relatively recent coinage dating from the 1970s, a *cruciverbalist* is someone who compiles or enjoys crosswords. The term is based on a literal Latin translation of the word 'crossword', and is formed from the Latin *crux*, meaning 'cross', and *verbum*, meaning 'word', presumably with some influence from the considerably older seventeenth-century term *verbalist*, describing someone who deals with or is particularly skilled in using words. *Cruciverbalism*, meanwhile, is a somewhat frivolous name for the compilation of crosswords first used in the 1990s.

3. JEU-DE-MOTS

Adopted from French, a *jeu-de-mots* is literally a 'game of words' – that is to say, a pun or similar instance of clever or witty wordplay. Dating from the early nineteenth century in English – the term was first recorded in Sir Walter Scott's 1823 novel *Peveril of the Peak* – *jeu-de-mots* is one of a number of unusual words and phrases used in English to describe wordplay, including *quiblin* and *quiblet*, literally 'small quibble' (early 1600s); *clench* (mid-1600s); *pundigrion* (late 1600s); and *calembour,* named after a clever wordsmith from traditional German folklore, the Abbé de Calemberg. The phrase *to play on words*, meanwhile, is taken from Shakespeare's *The Merchant of Venice* (III. v).

4. LECTURE

First used in English in the fourteenth century, the word *lecture* originally applied to either the actual action of reading or to what would now be known as *lection*, that is, how well a particular text or written work reads. It was not until the sixteenth century that the *lecture* came to be used to describe reading aloud, with the first reference to a specific spoken discourse delivered to an audience dating from the 1530s. The word itself is derived from the Latin word for 'reading', *lectura*, which is in turn descended from the Ancient Greek verb *legein*, meaning 'to speak', and ultimately the same root as the Greek *logos*, meaning 'speech' or 'word'.

5. LEXICOGRAPHY

Both *lexicography*, meaning 'writing or compilation of a dictionary', and *lexicon*, 'dictionary, or list of words', first appeared in English in the seventeenth century and derive from the same Ancient Greek root, *lexis*, meaning 'word', 'diction' or 'phrasing'. The same root is also the origin of a number of other English words, including the linguistic conditions *dyslexia*, first described in Germany in the 1870s; *paralexia*, in which words or syllables are substituted for one another while reading; and *alexia*, the name for a loss of the ability to comprehend language, coined in 1865.

6. LOGO

The word *logo* is a relatively recent addition to the English language dating from the early 1930s. It is believed to be an abbreviation of either one of two earlier words, *logogram* or *logotype*, both of which are ultimately descended from the Greek word for 'word', *logos*. A *logogram* is a sign or symbol used to represent a single word, as in symbol-based writing systems like those of Chinese, Japanese or Egyptian hieroglyphics, or else for brevity or speed in writing, such as the equals sign (=) and ampersand (&). A *logotype*, alternatively, was a printer's term for a combination of two or more letters – usually common sequences like 're', 'on', 'an' and 'th' – which could be cast from a single piece of type. Precisely of which one of these two words *logo* is the shortened form is unknown.

7. NAYWORD

Found in both *Twelfth Night* (II. iii) and *The Merry Wives of Windsor* (II. ii), *nayword* is a Shakespearean term thought to have had a number of different meanings including a 'proverb or saying', a 'catchphrase' and a 'byword'; perhaps its most literal meaning, however, is a 'password', as *nayword* is a contraction of the phrase 'an aye-word' (as in 'a yes word') implying that it would be used to be granted access to something that is otherwise kept secret. Other equally obscure terms formed from the word *word* include *hereword*, a 'term of praise' (c.1100); *bodeword*, a 'command' or 'message of instruction' (*c*.1200); *bug-word*, a 'word used to frighten, or said to tempt ill-fate' (mid-1500s); *non-word*, a 'word of no meaning', or a 'word unused until now' (late 1800s); *metaword*, a 'word used to describe another' in linguistics (1950s); and *fuzzword*, a 'term of deliberately misleading or ambiguous jargon' (1980s).

8. PALAVER

On its first appearance in the language in the 1700s, the word *palaver* originally referred to a quarrel or dispute or else to cajoling and persuasive chatter. Its more modern meaning of an 'uproar' or 'commotion' did not begin to appear until the late nineteenth century. The word's precise origin is unclear, but it seems likely that it was somehow adopted into English either from some West African Pidgin English or from nautical slang, yet in either case it is presumably based on the Portuguese word for 'word' or 'talk', *palavra*.

9. SCHIMPFWORT

Adopted from German in the 1940s, *schimpfwort* is a general name for an insult or term of abuse. It is a compound of the German words for 'insult', *schimpf*, and 'word', *wort*, but is usually considered a literal German translation of the English term 'swearword'. *Wort* appears in a handful of other words and phrases that have been at least partially adopted in English, although most tend only to be found in fairly obscure or specialized contexts: *wordsalat* (literally 'word salad'), for instance, was a phrase coined by the nineteenth-century German neurologist Carl Wernicke to describe the unintelligible language produced by patients who have suffered trauma to the language-processing part of the brain; *wortspiel* is literally a 'wordplay' or 'word game'; and, in linguistics, *wörter-und-sachen* is the name of a type of language study focusing on the regional dialect names of everyday 'words and things'.

10. VERB

Although in Modern English it is only used for words conveying an action or sense of being, the word *verb* derives from the Latin word *verbum*, which originally meant simply 'word'. This root is also the source of *adverb*, *proverb*, *biverb* (an odd term for a name comprising two words), *verbal* and even *verbicide*, an obscure nineteenth-century term for the misapplication of a word or the clumsy distortion of its meaning.

XIX

TEN WORDS DERIVED FROM NUMBERS

Besides familiar examples like *unicorn* (Latin *unus*, 'one'), *duet* (Latin *duo*, 'two') and *triangle* (Latin *tria*, 'three'), the English language contains a remarkably large collection of words that are derived from the names of numbers, ten of which are listed here. As well as examples like these, however, English is also home to a handful of terms that actually contain numbers or figures, many of which tend to be fairly recent coinages that originally developed as slang or idiomatic expressions. Describing something as *24–7*, for instance, comes from 1980s American slang, as does the expression the *411*, meaning 'information', which derives from the telephone number of the US directory enquiries. A *one-eighty* or *180* is a 1920s American term for a full reversal or retraction based on the notion of 180-degree turn, whilst to *eighty-six* or *86* has been used since the 1930s as a verb meaning to 'cancel', probably from American rhyming slang for 'nix'. The earliest of all words and phrases like these, however, is probably *one-two-three-four*, a mid-nineteenth-century name for a cake comprising one part butter, two parts sugar, three parts flour and four eggs.

1. DUODENUM
In human anatomy, the *duodenum* is the first section of the small intestine, connected to and lying immediately below the stomach. First used in English in the

97

fourteenth century, its somewhat unusual name stems from the Latin phrase *duodenum digitorum* – which is itself derived from *duodena*, the Latin word for a group of twelve – implying that the *duodenum* is typically 'twelve digits' (that is, twelve finger-breadths) in length.

2. KHAMSIN

The *khamsin* or *khamaseen* is a strong, hot and dry, south-to-south-easterly wind that blows from the Sahara into Egypt and the Arabian Peninsula in spring and early summer, often bringing with it vast sandstorms and dust-storms that can last for days on end. The word is based on the Arabic word for 'fifty', *khamsun*, as it is generally understood that the wind blows intermittently for a period of around fifty days beginning in late March.

3. MATATU

Literally meaning 'threes' in Swahili, the word *matatu* is believed to have been adopted into English from Kenya, where it is widely used as a name for an unlicensed minibus taxi. A major means of transportation in the most rural areas of Kenya and its surrounding countries, the word *matatu* is a shortened form of the Swahili phrase *mapeni matutu*, meaning 'three ten-cent coins', as thirty cents is seemingly a standard fare for the service the taxis provide.

4. MYRIAD

Typically used to suggest any large or innumerable amount of something (a sense first recorded in the mid-1500s), the word *myriad* originally strictly referred to a set of 10,000, and was used particularly in reference to a large hoard of solders or a quantity of money. In this sense, the word derives via Latin from the Ancient Greek word for '10,000', *myrias*, although this too could be used in some contexts to imply an infinite or unquantifiable amount. Use of the word as an adjective in English – as in 'myriad possibilities' or 'myriad combinations' – is a later development, dating from the early eighteenth century.

5. NOON

Despite its modern meaning, on its earliest appearance in the language in the Old English period the word *noon* originally applied to the ninth hour of the day after sunrise, usually reckoned to be around 3 p.m. This use of the word was adopted from the Romans and ultimately *noon* is derived from the Latin word for 'ninth', *nonus*, and in turn the Latin *novem*, meaning 'nine', from which *November* is also derived. Remarkably, *noon* did not come to apply to midday until as relatively recently as the thirteenth century, although quite what prompted the word's reallocation from 3 p.m. to 12 p.m. is unclear.

6. QUARANTINE

Referring to a period of isolation enforced on a person (or originally a ship) suspected of carrying an infectious disease, the word *quarantine* is derived from the Italian word for 'forty', *quarantina*, as this period of isolation was originally always forty days long. This medical use of the word dates from the mid-seventeenth century in English, but the term had in fact been in use in the language for several centuries before this meaning arose. Previously, *quarantine* was used in religious contexts to refer to the desert in which Jesus fasted for forty days and forty nights (1400s); in legal parlance to a period of forty days during which time a widow legally had the right to remain in her deceased husband's home (1500s); and it was once the name of a forty-day period of penance observed in the Christian Church (1600s). All of these older uses of the word derive directly from the Latin word for 'forty', *quadraginta*, from which English has also taken *quadragene*, a forty-day recession of punishment after confession in the Catholic Church, and *Quadragesima*, the forty days comprising Lent in the Christian calendar.

7. QUINQUEREME

Derived from the Latin words for 'five', *quinque*, and 'oar', *remus*, a *quinquereme* was a type of galley used in Ancient Greece and Rome that was powered by a vast number of oarsmen arranged into groups of five. Of similar derivation are the relatively more familiar terms *bireme* and *trireme* (with two and three ranks of oars, respectively), as well as the more obscure *pentereme* (another name for the *quinquereme*, derived from the Ancient Greek *pente*, 'five'), *octoreme* (a ship with eight men to each oar, from Latin *octo*, 'eight'), *penteconter* (an Ancient Greek vessel with fifty oars, from the Greek *pentekonta*, meaning 'fifty') and *tessarakonteres* (Greek *tessarakonta*, 'forty'), a gigantic galley supposedly built for Ptolemy Philopater of Egypt in the third century BC, thought to have had forty banks of oars.

8. SEPTUAGINT

Dating from the sixteenth century in English, in its earliest recorded sense the word *Septuagint* referred to the seventy Jewish translators who in the third century BC completed the first translation of the Hebrew Bible into Ancient Greek. According to some accounts – and contrary to the literal meaning of the word, given that *septuaginta* is the Latin word for 'seventy' – there were actually seventy-two translators involved, six from each of the twelve tribes of Israel. They supposedly completed the translation in seventy-two days at the request of King Ptolemy II Philadelphus of Egypt who wished for a copy of the text to be kept in the great library at Alexandria. In English, since the seventeenth century the word *Septuagint* has come to be used as an alternative name for the entire Greek version of the Old Testament, although this meaning is misleading given that at the time of the original translation the Old Testament would only have comprised the five books of the Jewish Pentateuch, namely Genesis, Exodus, Leviticus, Numbers and Deuteronomy.

9. TRIACONTARCHY

Triacontarchy literally means 'rule by thirty' and derives from the Ancient Greek words *triakonta*, meaning 'thirty', and *arkhein*, meaning 'to rule', the same root from which words like *monarchy*, *anarchy* and *hierarchy* are all also derived. Specifically, the word pertains to a period in the history of Ancient Greece when, following the victory of Sparta in the Peloponnesian War, a council of thirty pro-Spartan magistrates were put in control of Athens. Also referred to as the *oligarchy* (from the Greek *oligo*, meaning 'few'), these magistrates' short-lived rule was brought to an end by a bloody coup in 403 BC led by the exiled Greek general Thrasybulus, who overturned the council, killing several of its members in the process.

10. TRISKAIDEKAPHOBIA

First recorded in a 1911 work by the American psychologist Isador Coriat, *triskaidekaphobia* is the proper name for the irrational fear of the number thirteen, a phobia based on the superstitious belief amongst some cultures that the number is somehow unlucky. Derived from the

101

Ancient Greek word for 'thirteen', *treiskaideka*, the word is often also used to describe a superstitious fear of Friday the thirteenth, although the less well-established term *paraskevidekatriaphobia* (based on the Modern Greek word for 'Friday', *Paraskevi*) has recently been suggested as a more accurate name for that condition.

XX

TEN WORDS DERIVED FROM COLOURS

In English, most of the basic names for colours had equivalents in the Old English period, and are amongst the earliest of all words in the entire language, including *red* (Old English *read*), *yellow* (*geolwe*), *green* (*grene*), *blue* (*blaw*), *purple* (*purpul*), *black* (*blæc*), *white* (*hwit*), *grey* (*græg*) and *brown* (*brun*). Things only began being described as *orange*, meanwhile, in the sixteenth century after the fruit was introduced to England from the continent.

What remains baffling, however, is that only a handful of these words had equivalents in many of the most ancient languages, and notably Ancient Greek – in fact, so conspicuous is the absence of words for colours in the works of Greek writers like Homer and Sophocles that some nineteenth-century scholars theorized that the people of Ancient Greece had not yet developed the capacity to see in full colour, an idea famously championed by the classicist (and later British Prime Minister) William Gladstone in his 1858 work *Studies On Homer and the Homeric Age*. Historians today, however, tend to agree that the absence of the names for colours in a language does not necessarily demonstrate an inability of its speakers to recognize them, and it may simply be that such words were not considered important to writers at the time.

1. ALBEDO

In physics and astronomy, the term *albedo* describes the amount of light that is reflected back by a planetary body or surface, typically represented by a percentage of the total amount of light available; alternatively, in biology the term describes the white inner pith of a citrus fruit. *Albedo* is the Latin for 'whiteness', the sense by which the word first appeared in English in the eighteenth century, and is derived from *albus*, the Latin for 'white'. The words *albumen*, the scientific name for the white of an egg; *albino*, an organism lacking pigment in its skin; *alb*, a long, white tunic typically worn by religious officials; and *album*, which in its earliest sense referred to a Roman official's blank tablet, are all of similar origin.

2. BLANKET

First used in English in the early fourteenth century for a type of undyed woollen fabric, *blanket* is believed to be of French origin and is presumably a diminutive of the French word for 'white', *blanche*. Indeed, the verb *blanch*, the adjective *blank* and the food *blancmange*, made from whipped egg whites, are all of identical origin. Use of the word *blanket* to refer to a bedcover, meanwhile, dates from the fifteenth century, whilst as a verb meaning to 'cover' or 'protect' it was first used by Shakespeare in *King Lear* (II. iii): 'My face I'll grime with filth, / Blanket my loins, . . . / And with presented nakedness outface / The winds and persecutions of the sky.'

3. CHLORINE

The name of *chlorine* (Cl) – chemical element number 17 and the second lightest member of the halogen group – is derived from its colour. A strong-smelling, yellowish-green gas at room temperature, *chlorine* is a derivative of the Greek *chloros,* meaning 'pale green'. *Chloroform,* the organic compound once used as an anaesthetic, and *chlorophyll,* the structure that gives plants their green colour, are both derived from the same root. *Chlorine* is just one of several chemical elements to take its name from its colour, with others including *iodine* (Greek *ioeides,* 'violet'), *rubidium* (Latin *rubidus,* 'red'), *praseodymium* (Greek *prasios,* 'leek-green') and *zirconium* (thought to be derived from the Persian *zargun,* meaning 'golden').

4. CHRYSALIS

Referring to the case or sheath of hardened silk inside which a caterpillar or similar insect larva metamorphoses into an adult, the word *chrysalis* is derived from its equivalent Greek term *khrysallidos,* which is itself a derivative of the Greek *khrysos,* meaning 'gold' or 'golden-yellow'. The word *chrysanthemum* is of identical origin and literally means 'golden flower'.

5. DENIGRATE

The word *denigrate* dates from the late sixteenth century in English, and is descended from its Latin equivalent *denigrare.* Typically used to mean to 'defame' or 'degrade someone's character', the word in fact literally means to 'blacken' or 'darken', and is ultimately descended from the Latin word for 'black', *niger.* This literal use of the word was common in English in the seventeenth century, but has since fallen out of use along with a handful of related words including *denigrator,* another word for something that blackens or stains; *denigrature,* an eighteenth-century variant of *denigration*; and *dénigrement,* a nineteenth-century French loanword meaning 'ridicule' or 'disparagement'.

6. GRIZZLY

Although it is commonly used as another name for the North American brown bear, the word *grizzly* in fact derives from the French word for 'grey', *gris*. First recorded in the late sixteenth century, *grizzly* is a derivative of the much earlier fourteenth-century word *grizzle*, which was used both to describe anything grey-coloured or grey-haired and as a nickname for a grey-haired old man. Despite being predominantly brown, *grizzly bears* are thought to have gained their name from the grey-coloured tips to their fur, but it may be that the name is simply a misspelling of the adjective *grisly*, meaning 'gruesome' or 'unpleasant'.

7. MELANCHOLY

On its earliest use in English in the late fourteenth century, the word *melancholy* was a pseudo-medical term describing a condition characterized by ill-temperedness or depression supposedly brought on by a bodily excess of so-called 'black bile', one of the four humours of ancient physiology alongside blood, phlegm and choler. Derived via Latin from Ancient Greek, the word *melancholy* literally means 'black bile', and is formed from a compound of the Greek words *melanos* and *khole*. The Latin equivalents of these two roots – *ater*, 'black, murky', and *bilis*, 'bile' – are the origin of the similar English adjective *atrabilious*.

8. NILGAI

The *nilgai* is a species of antelope found throughout the Indian subcontinent and is the largest antelope native to Asia. Its name, first used in English in the late 1600s, literally means 'blue cow' (from the Sanskrit *nila*, meaning 'dark blue') as the male *nilgai* has a characteristic blue-grey coat. It is one of a vast number of animals to have been assigned names making reference their colour – *rorqual*, for instance, another name for the fin whale, is descended from a Scandinavian word, *rauðr*, meaning 'red'; the *dzeren*, a Mongolian antelope, takes its name from a local word meaning 'orange'; the *geelbek*, an Indian Ocean fish, has a name meaning 'yellow beak' in Afrikaans; and the *gillaroo*, a type of trout, takes its name from the Irish words for 'lad', *giolla*, and 'red', *ruadh*.

9. RUBRIC

The word *rubric* is derived from the Latin word *rubrica*, meaning 'red ink' or 'red ochre pigment', which is itself a derivative of the Latin word for 'red', *ruber*. First used in English in the early fifteenth century, the word has been used in a number of different senses over the years, most of which refer to instructions or guidelines that would have typically been written or printed in red ink. These include the directions on liturgical texts and prayer books (*c*.1400); section or chapter headings in official documents or legal statutes (early fifteenth century); and entries in lists or calendars of saints' days (late sixteenth century). The use of the word in reference to the instructions of a written examination is a more modern development first recorded in the 1950s.

10. VERDIGRIS

A greenish-blue, rust-like substance that forms on copper and copper alloys like brass and bronze, *verdigris* was first mentioned in English in the early fourteenth century. The term is derived from the twelfth-century French phrase *vert de Grèce*, literally meaning the 'green of Greece', perhaps in reference to its historical use as an artist's pigment, dating back to Ancient Greece.

XXI

TEN WORDS DERIVED FROM SHAPES

With the exception of some everyday terms like *triangle* and *square*, the majority of the proper names for geometric shapes – like *pentagon*, *hexagon* and *octagon* – are formed from compounds of Ancient Greek roots. In most cases, these names tend to follow the same pattern: the first part of the name is numerical, indicating the number of angles (and therefore sides) that the shape contains, whilst the second, the familiar *-gon* suffix, is a derivative of the Greek word for 'corner', *gonia*. This system can ultimately be used to create the names of an infinite number of shapes, from the smaller fifteen-sided *pentadecagon* (from *pentekaideka*, 'fifteen') and twenty-sided *icosagon* (*eikosa*, 'twenty') to the hundred-sided *hectogon* (*hekaton*, 'hundred') and thousand-sided *chiliagon* (*khilioi*, 'thousand'). Only a handful of these names ever make their way into dictionaries, however, as not all of them are of equal interest to mathematical study and, as the number of sides a shape increases, the more outlandish its name tends to be – a ninety-nine-sided shape, for instance, would be an *enneacontakaienneagon*.

I. AMPHIGORY
Amphigory, or *amphigouri*, is an unusual literary term for senseless or burlesque writing, or else a work of nonsense verse. Borrowed from French in the early nineteenth century, the word is believed to be formed from the Greek

prefix *amphi-*, meaning 'both' or 'around' (as in *amphibian*, a creature able to live both on land and in water), and *gyros*, the Greek word for 'circle'. If this were correct, *amphigory* would imply some sense of 'going around the circle', perhaps inferring that any attempt to understand such nonsensical writing is pointless and you will likely end up back where you started.

2. CADRE

Cadre is the French word for a picture frame or supporting framework, a sense that underpins most of the word's different uses in English. First recorded in the early nineteenth century as simply another word for a frame or structure, in the 1850s *cadre* gained a military association, referring to the basic framework of troops in a regiment, and a more specific use in the 1930s to describe a communist cell or faction. Borrowed directly from French into English, the word is descended from the Latin word *quadrum*, meaning 'square'.

3. CIRCUS

The first recorded use of the word *circus* in its most familiar sense of a circular arena for acrobats, clowns and other entertainers dates from 1791 in English, although throughout its history the word has also been used to refer to a bullring (1810s); a circular or semi-circular row of houses (1710s); a group of performing aircraft (1910s); and a riot or noisy uproar, a colloquial sense first used by Mark Twain in his 1869 travelogue *Innocents Abroad*. Originally, however, a *circus* was a large Roman amphitheatre used for spectacular public performances, exhibitions, races and other entertainments, of which Rome's *Circus Maximus* was the largest and grandest example. *Circus* is the Latin word for 'circle', as such buildings were typically circular in shape to allow for the best all-round views from the crowd.

4. DELTA

The familiar triangular shape of the upper-case letter *delta* (Δ), the fourth letter of the Greek alphabet, has ultimately led to its name being used metaphorically to refer to the triangular-shaped mouth of a river, a sense which at its earliest was used specifically to describe the mouth of the river Nile in the mid-sixteenth century. *Delta* is also the root of several other English words of a similar vein, including *deltoid,* a large triangular muscle found in the shoulder, and *deltidium,* the name for a small triangular space formed at the hinge of brachiopod shells.

5. GYROMANCY

Gyros, an Ancient Greek word for a circle or ring, is the origin of a number of English words including *gyroscope, gyrate,* and both *dextrogyrate* and *sinistrogyrate,* meaning 'turning to the right' and 'turning to the left' respectively. *Gyromancy,* meanwhile, is the name of an unusual form of divination dating from the sixteenth century in English, in which a person would walk around a circle of letters or symbols until they became dizzy and stumbled, with some significance then drawn from the point on the circle at which they fell.

6. QUADRATIC

The adjective *quadratic* is perhaps most familiar in English as the name of a type of algebraic equation, typically of the form $ax^2 + bx + c = 0$, in which x is an unknown and a, b and c are constants. *Quadratic* equations like this only ever deal with the second degree or 'square' of an unknown quantity – so x^2 is a *quadratic* form whereas x^3

(*cubic*) and x^4 (*quartic*) are not. The word is derived from the Latin for 'square', *quadratus*, and indeed on its first appearance in the language in the mid-seventeenth century, the adjective *quadratic* was used simply to describe things that are square or quadrangular in shape.

7. QUARRY

Both familiar uses of the word *quarry* – one describing the prey of a hunt and the other a large, open stone-works – date from the fourteenth century in English, but are derived from entirely different sources. In terms of hunting, *quarry* is descended from a Middle English word, *quirre*, used for the entrails of an animal which would be given to hounds as a reward for their hunt, which is ultimately descended from an Old French word, *cuir*, for the skin or hide of an animal. In reference to a stone-works, however, *quarry* is derived from its Latin equivalent *quarreria* or *quadraria*, which literally described a place where stones were 'squared' ready for use. In this context, *quarry* is descended from the Latin word for 'square', *quadrus*.

8. SQUADRON

The word *squadron* first appeared in the English language in the mid-sixteenth century and is believed to have been adapted from its Italian equivalent *squadrone*, which is a derivative of the Italian word for 'square', *squadra*. Initially, *squadron* referred to a small group of soldiers arranged in a square formation, but this specific use of the word has since been lost and the term has been used from the late 1570s onwards in English to refer simply to any small party or block of troops.

9. TESSELLATE

Dating from the late eighteenth century, the verb *tessellate* essentially means to 'make a mosaic', with the related

111

noun *tessellation* dating back to the mid-seventeenth century to describe a pattern or mosaic-like design comprised of a close-fitting arrangement of individual shapes. The word is derived from *tessella*, a diminutive of the earlier Latin term *tessera*, which was variously used to refer to a small square tile or counter, a six-sided die or, more specifically, to a small square or cube of wood or stone such as that which would be used to make a mosaic.

10. YUAN
First introduced in 1914, the *yuan* is the principal unit of currency of the People's Republic of China and has been used as the basis of the country's so-called *renminbi* currency system since it was established in 1948. Divided into ten *jiao*, and in turn into a hundred *fen*, the name *yuan* means literally 'circle' or 'round' in Chinese, and is also the origin of the Japanese *yen*.

XXII

TEN WORDS DERIVED FROM FOOD

The ten words listed here are all descended from the name of a different food or drink, from basics like milk, rice and salt, to the name of a type of stew, a slang word for potatoes and an old name for the pomegranate. Of all food-related words in the language, however, it is probably *bread* that is the most productive as, besides COM-PANION and its related forms listed below, the Latin word for 'bread', *panis*, is also the root of a vast and intriguing collection of less familiar words including *apanage*, a gift of land or royal entitlement bestowed as a birthright; *impanation*, a term from Christianity for the embodiment of Christ in the Eucharist; *panatela*, a long, thin cigar, named after an Italian biscuit; *pannam-fencer*, an English dialect word for a street vendor or fairground stall, selling cakes and other confectionaries; and *marchpane*, an old-fashioned, sixteenth-century English name for marzipan. *Marzipan* itself is believed to take its name from that of the Burmese port of Martaban, which was once world-renowned for its production of jars and pots.

I. BAHUVRIHI

In linguistics, the Sanskrit term *bahuvrihi* is used to describe a certain type of compound word in which the second part is characterized by, or else possesses a quality implied by, the first – such as *bluebell*, *highbrow* or *redhead*. Typically, compounds of this type are classed as 'exocentric', meaning that neither of the words involved actually denotes what the compound itself means (so a *birdbrain* is neither a 'bird' nor a 'brain', but a foolish person) and indeed *bahuvrihi* is an example of just this type of word, being a compound of the Sanskrit words *bahú*, meaning 'much', and *vrihí*, meaning 'rice'.

2. BARAGOUIN

The odd word *baragouin* is another word for gibberish or unintelligible language or speech, adopted into English in the early 1600s from French, where the word is still used today to refer contemptuously to speech or writing containing a lot of technical jargon. *Baragouin* is descended from the Breton language of northern France and is formed from the local words for 'bread', *bara*, and 'wine', *gwin*, although quite how it developed is unclear. One popular suggestion maintains that the word probably originated amongst French innkeepers who were unable to understand Breton-speaking travellers asking for *bara* and *gwin*.

3. COMPANION

Adopted into English from French, the word *companion* has been used in English since the late thirteenth century. Historically, it derives from the Latin *companionem*, formed from the prefix *com-*, meaning 'with' or 'together', and *panis*, the Latin word for 'bread'. As such it is likely that the earliest sense of the word was that of a 'frequent dinner companion' or else a 'messmate' in the army. The words *company* and *accompany* are both of similar derivation, as is *pantry*, originally specifically used to describe a room in which bread was stored.

4. GALAXY

Adopted from French, the word *galaxy* was first used in English in the late fourteenth century and is descended, via Latin, from the Greek word *galaxias*. In this original form, the word literally means 'milky' (from Greek *galaktos*, 'milk', as in *lactose* and *lactation*) and was initially only used in reference to our own galaxy, the Milky Way or *via lactea*, which Greek astronomers first identified as a faint white band of stars that encircled the night sky – according to Greek myth, these stars were formed by a spray of milk from the breast of the goddess Hera. It was not until the late seventeenth century that the word came to be used for any of the billions of galaxies contained in the universe, and not just our own.

5. GRENADE

Remarkably, the first use of the word *grenade* in English to refer to an explosive or incendiary weapon dates from as far back as 1591, and indeed similar devices containing a mixture of flammable chemicals known as 'Greek fire' are known to have been used by troops of the Byzantine Empire in the eighth century. The word itself comes from *granade*, an English word for the pomegranate dating from the sixteenth century (and derived from the Spanish *granada*) as the shape of the fruit is said to be similar to that of early grenade-like devices.

6. HOTCHPOTCH

Meaning 'jumble' or 'disorganized medley', both the fifteenth-century word *hotchpotch* and its later seventeenth-century equivalent *hodgepodge* are thought to have developed from *hotchpot*, the name of a type of stew containing a mixture of numerous different ingredients first described in the thirteenth century. It turn, *hotchpot* is likely to be a development of the earlier French *hochepot*, a similar stew of minced beef and vegetables dating from the early 1200s. Oddly, this French term was also used in legal parlance for a merging of property, a sense thought to come from the Old French verb *hochier*, meaning 'to jostle' or 'to shake to and fro'.

7. MONOPSONY
The term *monopsony* was coined in a 1933 work by the acclaimed English economist Joan Robinson, who in turn credited the word to her fellow economist and Cambridge scholar Bertrand Hallward. It applies to a market situation in which there is only one buyer or consumer for a given commodity, and as such is formed from the Greek prefix *mono-*, meaning 'one' or 'alone', and *opsonein*, essentially meaning 'to buy provisions' or 'to cater for'. Along with a handful of similar and equally obscure words like *opsonation* ('feast', 'provision of food') and *opsony* (an odd seventeenth-century term for any food eaten with bread), *monopsony* is related to the Ancient Greek word *opson*, a general term for any relish or flavoursome delicacy (and in particular fish) which would be served alongside the main body of a meal.

8. PATOOTIE
First recorded in 1921, the word *patootie* began as an American slang term for an attractive girl, or more specifically a girlfriend or sweetheart, before later developing into a humorous name for the buttocks, a sense also found in the shortened forms *patoot* and *tootie* in the 1940s. The word's origins are unclear, but it has been suggested that it is simply a jocular alteration of the word 'potato', perhaps implying a pun on the 'sweet potato'.

9. RESTAURANT
Given that it is such a familiar word today, it is surprising that the word *restaurant* is a relatively recent addition to the English language and dates back no further than the

early nineteenth century. In its native French, however, the word dates from the early fifteenth century, when it was used to describe any food or consumable that had a fortifying or recuperative effect, restoring health or strength to the person who consumes it; in particular, in the mid-1600s, it was used to describe a type of hearty, meat-filled broth.

10. SALARY

Use of the word *salary* to mean a regular payment made in return for work dates from the late fourteenth century in English, when it specifically applied to the income of a priest. The word itself, however, is considerably older than that and derives via French from the Latin *salarium*, the name applied to money given to Roman soldiers for the purchase of salt or *sal*; contrary to popular belief, Roman soldiers were not actually paid in salt. This original meaning has long since vanished from the word *salary* itself, but is still maintained in the expression *to be worth one's salt*, which dates from the nineteenth century.

XXIII

TEN WORDS DERIVED FROM CLOTHING

Whilst the ten words listed here are all derived from the names of specific garments, more general references to clothing in the English language can be found in a vast number of phrases and idiomatic expressions. *To wear the trousers* or *to wear the pants*, for instance, has been used since the nineteenth century to imply that someone is the more dominant member of a household or relationship. *To be caught with your trousers down*, in an embarrassing or compromising situation, dates from the 1920s, as does the expression *not in these trousers!*, meaning 'no chance!', whilst *to fly by the seat of your pants* is a 1930s phrase originally used in reference to pilots who were able to monitor or guide an aeroplane by feeling its movement through their legs. Amongst the earliest of all such expressions, however, are those that use the word *shirt* as a metaphor for all of a person's belongings – to *not have a shirt*, meaning to 'have absolutely nothing', is found in Chaucer's *The Canterbury Tales* as far back as the fourteenth century.

1. BERSERK

Historically, *berserks* or *berserkers* were wild Scandinavian warriors known for their considerable strength and ferociousness. First mentioned in English in the early nineteenth century (in a collection of traditional Scandinavian sagas partly compiled by Sir Walter Scott), the word *berserker* is thought to mean literally 'bear-shirt' or 'bearskin coat', derived from an Old Norse word *serkr*, meaning 'shirt' or 'pelt'. Shortened to *berserk* in the mid-nineteenth century and first used as an adjective meaning 'frenzied' or 'out of control' in the 1850s, the word eventually began to appear in the familiar phrase *go berserk*, meaning 'go wild', in the 1910s.

2. CAPPUCCINO

It is fairly well known that the word *cappuccino* is thought to derive from the name of the sixteenth-century Capuchin friars of Italy, whose robes were said to be of a similar colour to the coffee. The Capuchins themselves, however, take their name from *cappuccio*, the Italian name for the sharp-pointed hood or cowl they wear as part of their robes, which is descended from the same root as the English word *cap*. Likewise, *capuchin* monkeys native to South America are so named as their dark-coloured heads are said to resemble the monks' cowls.

3. CHAPERON

In the sense of an accompanying guardian or protector, the word *chaperon* was first recorded in English in the early 1700s. Before this, it had been used since the early fourteenth century as the name of a type of hood or cap partly covering the face, and is derived directly from the identical French words for 'hood', *chaperon*, and 'cape', *chape*. The connection between this original meaning and the more contemporary one is debatable, but it could simply be a figurative reference to the fact that a *chaperon* protects the person in their care in much the same way as a hood gives protection from the rain.

4. COTILLION

A *cotillion* is an intricate ballroom dance, similar to a quadrille, in which four or more couples dance in squares. Originating in France in the eighteenth century, the dance takes its name from the French word for a petticoat, *cotillon*, which is itself a diminutive of the earlier French word *cote* or *cotte*, meaning 'coat'. In British English, the word is rarely encountered outside historical contexts today, but it has survived in American English as another word for a formal ball or prom dance, in which sense it was first used in the late 1800s.

5. DISMANTLE

Adopted into English from the old French verb *desmanteller*, the word *dismantle* dates from the late sixteenth century when it was originally used in military or defensive contexts to refer to the destruction of a fortress or similar structure, rendering it useless. The word itself, however, literally means 'remove a cloak', and is derived from the same root as *mantle*, an old-fashioned English word for a cape or loose sleeveless robe, which has been recorded as far back as the ninth century.

6. HACKLE

At its very earliest, the word *hackle* is found as *hacele* in the early Old English period in reference to a type of cloak or similar outer garment. Over time, use of the word broadened so as to refer more generally to any protective covering or casing, and it gained a number of different senses referring to the plumage of a bird (1400s), the shed skin of a serpent (*c.*1500s), the straw roof of a beehive (1600s) and the topmost straw of a haystack or hayrick (1600s). *Raise your hackles* or *put your hackles up*, meaning 'angered' or 'enraged', both date from the late nineteenth century and derive from the use of the word to refer to the long quills or plumes found on the back of a cockerel's neck, which are typically raised up when the bird is angered or attacked.

7. LAP

The word *lap* is one of the oldest traceable words in the entire English language and has been recorded in documents dating back as far as the ninth century. Remarkably, the use of the word to describe the level space formed between the waist and the knees when sitting did not appear in English until the late thirteenth century, almost 400 years later. Before this, *lap* was used to refer to a fold or flap in a garment, and in particular one which could be held up or folded over so as to form a pouch, like the skirt of a coat or the part of a robe or shirt that covers the chest. Subsequently, the word came to be used for any pocket or pouch-like appendage (it is even recorded as another name for the earlobe in an eleventh-century text), and ultimately the modern sense of the word is thought to have developed from the use of the *lap* to hold or cradle something in much the same way as a pouch.

8. MANTA

Found in deep tropical seas around the world, the giant *manta* or 'devilfish' is the largest species of ray in the world, typically growing to more than 7 m (23 ft) across. The name *manta* is of Spanish origin and literally means 'blanket', but is ultimately derived from the Latin word for a cloak or cape, *mantum.* In English, the word was first recorded in the mid-1700s in *A Voyage to South America,* an English translation of the travel journals of the Spanish explorer and astronomer Antonio de Ulloa, who aptly explains that 'The name manta, has not been improperly given to this fish . . . for being broad and long like a quilt, it wraps its fins round a man or any other animal . . . and immediately squeezes it to death'. Although Ulloa's description of the creature's appearance is accurate, his portrayal of its apparently ferocious hunting method is mistaken, as mantas are in fact filter feeders that only consume plankton and tiny fish larvae. Despite being closely related to sharks, they pose no threat to humans.

9. TAWDRY

Meaning 'cheap' or 'gaudy', *tawdry* was first used in English in the late 1600s, but the word itself dates from the first half of the seventeenth century when it was used as the name of a type of lady's necktie, typically made from so-called *tawdry lace*. The word is formed from a contraction of the name of 'St Audrey', a seventh-century Suffolk-born Queen of Northumbria and a former abbess of Ely in Cambridgeshire, where for many years an annual fair was held in her honour. According to local lore, St Audrey died of a tumour to her throat in 679 (a condition which she considered divine retribution for her fondness for showy necklaces in her youth) and so after her death lace neckties and bands were sold at Ely in her memory. When these ties became increasingly popular in the sixteenth and seventeenth century many poor-quality imitations were produced, which ultimately lent the word *tawdry* the meaning it still bears today.

10. TULIP

A popular spring-flowering plant of the lily family, the *tulip* was first recorded in English in the late sixteenth century. Presumably adopted into the language from one of several possible continental sources – including the French *tulipe* or the Dutch *tulpe* – the word *tulip* is ultimately derived via Turkish from the Persian word for a turban, *dulband*, which the plant's somewhat bulbous and colourful flower-heads are said to resemble.

XXIV

TEN WORDS DERIVED FROM MUSIC

The vast majority of musical terms and directions used in English are of Italian origin, as many of the principal composers of the baroque and Renaissance periods who established much of what now forms the basis of classical music were Italian, including Palestrina, Monteverdi, Pergolesi and Vivaldi. Italian loanwords dominate lists of musical compositions and performances (*concerto, opera, sonata*), musical instruments (*piano, tuba, viola, piccolo*) and voices (*soprano, contralto, alto*), as well as performance instructions describing variables like speed (*tempo, allegro, presto*) and volume (*forte, crescendo, diminuendo*). Italian terms are also used to give character to a piece of music, explaining how it should feel or sound – pieces marked *agitato, animato* and *maestoso*, for instance, should sound 'agitated', 'animated' and 'majestic', respectively. Others dictate how an instrument should be played, like *pizzicato*, telling a player to pluck the strings, and *con legno*, indicating that a string should be played with the wooden part of a bow.

1. AD-LIB

An abbreviation of the Latin phrase *ad libitum*, meaning 'at one's pleasure' (a form of the same verb, *libire*, from which *libido* is also derived), the word *ad-lib* has a variety of senses in English, amongst the earliest of which is its use as a musical term indicating that a corresponding passage of music is optional and need not necessarily be performed. Dating from the mid-1700s, in this context the word *ad-lib* was often applied to a musical part written for an instrument that could be excluded from an ensemble if need be. In more modern compositions the term tends to be used to indicate that a piece can be played in whatever way the performer sees fit, or else that some part of it can be improvised or embellished at the performer's discretion. The more general use of *ad-lib* to refer to a spontaneous or unplanned remark dates from the early nineteenth century, whilst the use of *ad-lib* as a verb was first recorded in 1910.

2. BAZOOKA

As the name of a type of portable rocket launcher, the word *bazooka* was first used in English in 1943. Before this, the *bazooka* was originally a musical instrument, a large, rudimentary wind instrument similar to a trombone, which was invented in the early 1900s by Bob Burns, an American comedian and radio star who went on to become one of the most popular US entertainers of the Second World War. Burns constructed his original *bazooka* (a derivative of *bazoo*, a slang name for the mouth) from two lengths of gas pipe and a funnel. When the US military's portable M1 anti-tank rocket-launcher was introduced in 1942 American troops soon nicknamed it the *bazooka* due to its apparent similarity to Burns's invention.

3. DOWNBEAT

Dating from the mid-nineteenth century, the musical term *downbeat* is used to describe the strongest or most heavily accented beat of a bar of music, so called as it would be the beat on which a conductor would bring the baton downwards, before a subsequent *upbeat*. Quite how the term gained a later adjectival sense meaning 'gloomy', 'unpretentious' or 'subdued', however, is unclear but it is perhaps simply due to the somewhat negative connotations of the word *down*.

4. FINALE

Borrowed into English from Italian in the mid-1700s, the word *finale* was originally a musical term, used to denote the concluding movement of an opera, symphony or similarly lengthy composition, before gaining an extended figurative use in the nineteenth century for any grand ending or conclusion. The word is descended from the Latin word *finalis*, meaning 'final', and ultimately *finis*, meaning 'end' or 'limit', and as such is related to other English words including *infinity*, *define* and *affinity*.

5. GAMUT

The word *gamut* dates from the early sixteenth century in English and is formed from a contraction of the Latin *gamma-ut*, the name given to the lowest note on the medieval musical scale which now corresponds to the second G below middle C. Historically, the Greek letter *gamma* was used to represent this bass G, while *ut* was used as the first syllable of the *solfège* or *sol-fa*, the scaled series of musical syllables that now usually begins *do, re, mi*. Over time, the use of the word *gamut* broadened to refer not just to the lowest note on the scale but to the entire range of the scale itself, and by the seventeenth century it had begun to be used figuratively to refer to the full scope or range of anything, the meaning by which it is almost exclusively used today.

6. HYDRAULIC

As an adjective referring to the action of water or other fluids moving through pipes, the word *hydraulic* dates from the 1660s. It is derived via the Latin *hydraulicus*, a word used by the Romans for various water-propelled engines, from the Greek words *hydor*, meaning 'water', and *aulos*, meaning 'pipe' or 'flute'. The word is ultimately related to the Ancient Greek *hydraulis*, a type of water organ said to have been invented by the Greek engineer Ctesibius in the third-century BC, which used a mixture of air and water pressure to produce its sound. The *hydraulis* is considered by some to have been the first keyboard instrument in the history of music.

7. MELODRAMA

The word *melodrama* was adopted into English from Italian in the late eighteenth century as a musical term referring to a spoken dramatic performance accompanied by songs or music, or else a section of a much larger musical composition, like an opera, during which instrumental music is played to accompany a spoken passage or speech. Beethoven's opera *Fidelio* (1805) features perhaps the most well-known *melodrama* in all classical music, although other famous examples include a similar passage in Benjamin Britten's opera *Peter Grimes* (1945), and Richard Strauss's musical adaptation of the Tennyson poem 'Enoch Arden' (1897). The more general use of *melodrama* to refer to a sensational or overly dramatic scene dates from the early nineteenth century.

8. KEYNOTE

In music, the *keynote* is the first and lowest note of a musical scale (also known as the *tonic*), which establishes the tonality or key of the notes that follow it. The word dates from the late 1600s in English, but since the mid-1700s has been used in a broader metaphorical sense to refer to the tone or principle behind an argument or discussion. In this context, *keynote* is most often found today as part of the expression *keynote speech* or *keynote address,* a phrase originating in American English in the early twentieth century, which typically refers to the opening speech of a conference which outlines the focus of the meeting as a whole.

9. SEGUE

Used generally to denote a smooth transition or movement from one situation to another, the word *segue* was originally purely a musical term of equivalent meaning, instructing a performer to move seamlessly from one section or piece of music to the next. Like most musical directions, the word was adopted into English from Italian, and literally means 'follows'. It was first recorded in English in the mid-1700s, but in a general sense of 'seamless movement' dates from the 1950s.

10. TELEPHONE

What we consider a *telephone* dates back in the English language to the 1870s and the development of numerous electrical communication devices by inventors including Alexander Graham Bell, Thomas Edison and Elisha Gray. The word *telephone* itself, however – a compound of the Greek *telos*, meaning 'far', and *phone,* meaning 'sound' – is considerably older. In fact, it dates back as far as the 1830s to a device created by the eighteenth- to nineteenth-century French musician and inventor Jean-François Sudré that used musical notes as a means of relaying messages across distances. Sudré, who had earlier devised an artificial language named *Solresol* that used combinations of musical notes to spell out words, first demonstrated his musical *téléphone* in the 1820s, with the first written record of his 'telephone system' dating from 1835, predating Bell's invention by some forty years.

XXV

TEN WORDS DERIVED FROM
THE THEATRE

The ten words listed here are all either derived from specific theatrical terms or were originally used in theatrical contexts before developing broader, more general uses elsewhere in the language. Besides these, English also contains a number of words that have been adopted into drama or acting, or that have gained a new meaning in the theatre or on the stage. The word *apron*, for instance, dates from the fourteenth century as the name of a protective garment, but came to be used to describe a kind of stage, first popular in the Elizabethan period, that projects outwards so as to be surrounded by the audience on all sides. To *corpse* has been theatrical slang (in the sense of 'murdering' a scene) since the mid-1800s and refers either to an actor forgetting their lines or laughing at an inopportune time during a performance. And a *limelight* was originally a specific device invented in the 1820s that comprised a stick of quicklime (calcium oxide) burnt in a flame of combined hydrogen and oxygen to produce a particularly intense light. In the mid-nineteenth century, the popular use of a *limelight* as a spotlight for the lead actors in theatre ultimately led to the term becoming a byword for fame or celebrity.

I. BACKGROUND
Although it is today used in a variety of different contexts and senses, the earliest meaning of the word *background*

comes from the theatre, where it was originally used to refer to the rear part of a stage, lying furthest from the audience. Indeed, the first recorded use of the word in English comes from a stage direction in the Restoration comedy *Love in a Wood* (1671) by the Elizabethan writer William Wycherley. Over time, use of the word *background* broadened and it became a much less specialized term, referring first to the scenery or setting of a painting in the mid-1700s; then to any disconnected or inconspicuous position in the late 1700s; and lastly to a person's upbringing or family history in the early 1900s. The first known reference to *background music*, meanwhile, dates from 1928.

2. BARNSTORMING
In modern English, the word *barnstorming* tends to be used as an adjective, typically describing anything such as a speech or performance that is particularly boisterous or theatrical. The original *barnstormers* were nineteenth-century itinerant actors and performers in the United States, who would travel around the countryside stopping intermittently to put on stage shows, expositions and entertainments in barns and similar large buildings. Use of the word soon spread to politics, with *barnstorming* first used in reference to an electioneering tour in the late 1890s.

3. BLACKOUT
The earliest use of the word *blackout* in English was a purely theatrical one, used to refer to the darkening of the stage between the scenes or acts of a play. In this context, the word was first recorded in a letter written by George Bernard Shaw to his producer and director Granville Barker in 1913, in which he makes reference to a production of his play *Androcles and the Lion*. In the

decades that followed, *blackout* gained several additional figurative meanings, all developed from this original sense of the word, including 'temporary loss of vision, consciousness or memory' (1920s–30s); 'widespread power failure' (1930s); 'precautionary shielding or extinguishing of lights during air raids' (1930s); 'intentional suppression of the media, or news reporting' (1940s); and 'period during which a certain product or commodity is not available' (1950s).

4. CATASTROPHE

Used more loosely since the mid-1700s to describe any great disaster or calamity, the word *catastrophe* was originally a dramatic term used to refer to the point in a story or plot at which an event occurs – not necessarily a tragic or disastrous one – that will ultimately bring about the final conclusion of the piece. The word was first used in this sense in English in the late sixteenth century, but it has its origins in the theatre of Ancient Greece and is derived from a Greek term, *katastrophe*, literally meaning 'a turn against'.

5. EXPLODE

First recorded in the early seventeenth century, the word *explode* originally meant to 'clap or jeer a performer off the stage'. The term derives from the equivalent Latin term *explaudere*, which is in turn a derivative of the same Latin verb – *plaudere*, meaning 'to clap' – from which the English words *applaud* and *plaudit* are both also derived. Over time, *explode* developed a number of other meanings, including to 'reject' (mid-1500s); to 'mock' or 'deride' (early 1600s); to 'expel' or 'drive out noisily' (late 1600s); and eventually to 'burst' or 'combust with a loud noise', a sense first recorded in the late 1700s.

6. HOKUM

Probably partly based on the earlier term *bunkum*, with perhaps some influence from *hocus-pocus*, *hokum* first appeared in the United States in early 1900s when it was used amongst actors and theatre practitioners to describe any overly melodramatic speech or dramatic device used to provoke a reaction amongst the audience. Over time, its meaning broadened to come to refer to anything seemingly impressive or meaningful but actually of little real worth, and ultimately to the more familiar sense of 'nonsense' or 'garbage' by which it is most often used today. Other words to have developed from actors' slang include *patsy*, a term for a deceived party or scapegoat, dating from the late nineteenth century; *mug*, meaning 'pull exaggerated faces', first recorded in Dickens's *Little Dorrit* in 1856; and *swipe*, in the sense of 'steal', thought to have originated amongst American entertainers in the nineteenth century who would 'swipe' jokes from other performers' acts.

7. HYPOCRISY

The word *hypocrisy* was first recorded in English as far back as the thirteenth century. Believed to have entered the language from French, it is derived from the Greek *hypokrisis*, a theatrical term which referred to the acting of a role on the stage, and is based on the Greek *hypokrinesthai*, variously meaning 'to act', 'to decide' or 'to answer'.

8. MACHINERY

The earliest use of the word *machinery* in English was in reference to the devices and apparatus used in a theatre to create various effects on stage; first recorded in the 1680s, it was not until the mid-1700s that use of the word became generalized to refer to any collection of machines or mechanisms. The original 'god in the machine' or *deus ex machina*, meanwhile, was the Greek *theos ek mekhanes*, a device used to suspend actors playing gods above the stage during a performance. Eventually, the phrase came to refer to the resolution of a plot through the last-minute introduction of a character or event, a sense first recorded in English in the late seventeenth century.

9. PROTAGONIST

The root of the word *protagonist* is the Greek theatrical term *protagonistes* – a compound of *protos*, meaning 'first', and *agonistes*, meaning a 'combatant' or 'competitor' – which was used in Ancient Greek theatre to refer to the lead actor in a dramatic performance. On its first appearance in English in the late 1600s, *protagonist* was also used exclusively to describe the lead or central character in a story, but over time its use has been generalized to come to refer to any prominent person or figurehead, or else simply to a supporter or advocate of a particular cause. Of similar origin is *antagonist*, which originally applied to an opponent in a battle or game, whilst the related forms *deuteragonist* and *tritagonist* are used to describe the second and third most important actors in a performance.

10. SHOWBOAT

First recorded in American English in 1869, a *showboat* was originally literally that – a riverboat or paddle steamer that staged theatrical shows and entertainments on board. Based on this original meaning, the word was adapted into a verb in twentieth-century American slang, meaning to 'show-off' or 'grandstand', and then back into a noun in the 1950s to refer to someone who courts public attention through conspicuous or exhibitionist behaviour.

XXVI

TEN WORDS DERIVED FROM
LITERARY CHARACTERS

It is probably Charles Dickens who above all other writers
has contributed the most characters to the language, with
more than twenty of his creations – including such
recognizable figures as *Scrooge* ('miser'), *Micawber* ('opti-
mist') and *Fagin* ('thief') – now listed as entries in the
Oxford English Dictionary. The cold-hearted headmaster
Thomas Gradgrind in *Hard Times* has given his surname
to anyone similarly cold or unyielding; a *Stiggins* is
defined as a 'pious humbug', taken from the surname of
the Reverend Stiggins in *The Pickwick Papers*; and a
Gummidge is a pessimistic grumbler, named after the dour
widow in *David Copperfield*. Some of Dickens's characters
have even produced their own derivatives in English,
including *Tapleyism*, meaning 'unfaltering optimism',
derived from Mark Tapley in *Martin Chuzzlewit*; *bumbledom*,
meaning 'pomposity' or 'officiousness', named after the
self-important beadle Mr Bumble in *Oliver Twist*; and
WELLERISM, listed here.

I. BRAINIAC

A combination of *brain* and *maniac*, the word *brainiac*
derives from the name of a devious, super-intelligent
adversary of Superman who first appeared in *The Super-
Duel in Space*, one of DC Comics's 'Action Comics' series
printed in 1958. One of Superman's most memorable

enemies, the name *brainiac* eventually slipped into more general use in English in the 1970s, and was first recorded as nickname for an extremely intelligent or geekish person in 1975.

2. CELADON
The name of both a pale grey-green colour and a type of green porcelain originally produced in China, the word *celadon* is thought to derive from Céladon, the name of a character who habitually dressed in pale green ribbons in *L'Astrée* (1627), a work by the sixteenth- to seventeenth-century French writer Honoré d'Urfé. In turn, d'Urfé is believed to have adopted the name from a character mentioned in Ovid's *Metamorphoses*, namely a guest at the wedding of Andromeda of whom no mention is made other than to say that he is killed by Perseus.

3. HARLEQUIN
First recorded in English in 1590, Harlequin was one of the stock characters of English pantomime who was adopted from French comic theatre and the popular *commedia dell'arte* of Italy in the sixteenth century. In English theatrical tradition, Harlequin is usually depicted as a clown or mime, armed with a wooden sword or wand, and dressed in a ludicrously garish costume – indeed, the word *harlequin* has been used as an adjective meaning 'variegated' or 'multi-coloured' since the eighteenth century.

4. LOTHARIO
The name *Lothario* seems to have enjoyed a long-standing association with lecherous characters in literature that probably began with 'The Impertinent Curiosity', the story-within-the-story retold in Cervantes's *Don Quixote*

(1605–15), in which Lothario is an unscrupulous rake who is coerced into seducing another man's wife to test her fidelity. In turn, this Lothario is thought to have inspired another who appeared in Sir William Davenant's play *The Cruel Brother* (1630), and yet another who featured in *The Fair Penitent* (1703) by the English dramatist Nicholas Rowe. It is Rowe's play that is credited with popularizing the word as another name for a seducer of women in English in the mid-eighteenth century.

5. PANTALOONS

The sixteenth-century word *pantaloons* derives from the name of Pantaloon or Pantalone, a stock character of French and Italian comic theatre who is typically depicted as a scrawny, hunchbacked old man, dressed in long red tights (his *pantaloons*), a long black cloak or jacket and a hat. In the original Italian *commedia dell'arte*, Pantalone was often portrayed as the embodiment of greed, a rich yet miserly old widower or bachelor. His name was likely taken from that of St Pantaleon, one of the saints of the Republic of Venice, as at the time Venetian merchants were widely known for their prosperity.

6. POINDEXTER

Describing a bookish and often socially inept young man, the word *poindexter* was first recorded in English in 1981. It derives from the name of a character who first appeared in the popular US animated series *Felix the Cat* in 1959. A nerdy nephew of the Professor, Felix's adversary, Poindexter was portrayed as a short young boy wearing a mortar board, thick round glasses and a lab coat. According to the show's producer and animator Joe Oriolo, the character was named after his lawyer.

7. RODOMONTADE

The word *rodomontade* is used in English to mean 'boastful, pretentious blather', or else is used as another name for a vain and bragging person. First recorded in this sense in the late sixteenth century, the word was borrowed via French from the Italian *Rodomonte*, the name of a pompous, arrogant character in the epic Renaissance poem *Orlando Innamorato* (*Orlando in Love*) written in the late 1400s.

8. STRUWWELPETER

The title character in a children's story written by the German writer Heinrich Hoffmann, the name *Struwwelpeter* is used in English to describe someone with unkempt and uncontrollable hair, a sense first recorded in 1909. In the original tale, Struwwelpeter (usually translated into English as 'tousle-headed Peter') is a young boy who 'never once has cut his hair' or his fingernails which are long and 'grimed as black as soot'. His is one of several stories – along with those of 'Cruel Frederick', a boy who tears the wings off flies, and 'The Wild Huntsman', who is hunted by a hare who has stolen his gun – which Hoffmann originally published in a collection known as *Merry Stories and Funny Pictures* in 1845.

9. SVENGALI

The word *Svengali* has been used in English to describe a person who has control or influence over another, particularly via some sinister or mesmeric means, since the early 1900s. It is taken from the name of a villainous character in *Trilby* (1894), a novel by the French writer and cartoonist George du Maurier (grandfather of the English authoress Daphne du Maurier). In the story Svengali is a great musician and hypnotist who transforms

the title character into a magnificent and hugely successful singer, but leaves her utterly unable to perform without his powers and ultimately asserts complete control
over her life.

10. WELLERISM

A *Wellerism* is a type of expression in which an existing saying or cliché is given a humorously alternative meaning
by being placed in an unusual context. The term is
derived from the name of the popular character of Sam
Weller, Mr Pickwick's witty manservant in Dickens's *The
Pickwick Papers* (1837), who would typically make obser-
vations (in his cockney accent) like '[what] I call addin'
insult to injury, as the parrot said ven they not only took
him from his native land, but made him talk the English
langvidge arterwards'. The term *Wellerism* was first
recorded in English just two years after publication of *The
Pickwick Papers* in 1839, indicating just how popular a
character Sam was amongst Dickens's readership. Indeed,
when the novel was first serialized in monthly instalments
from March 1836 to October 1837, sales reportedly
increased from 500 to 40,000 a month after Sam made
his first appearance in Chapter 10.

XXVII

TEN WORDS DERIVED FROM
GREEK MYTHOLOGY

References to the Greek myths are more common in the English language than might be expected, with some of the most familiar of English words having their origins in names of legendary Greek characters. *Morphine*, for instance, derives its name from Morpheus, the Greek god of dreams; the adjective *erotic* literally pertains to the Greek god of love, Eros; and even *calypso* music shares its name with that of a wily sea nymph in Homer's *Odyssey*. Similarly, expressions such as a *Herculean task* and an *Achilles heel* date back many centuries in the language, with Chaucer referencing the 'strengthe of Ercules' in *The Book of the Duchess* written *c.*1369, and a medical textbook of 1703 describing 'That String . . . call'd the Tendon of Achilles, because, 'tis said, he dy'd of a Wound in that Part'. Perhaps the most familiar of all such words, however, is *atlas*, which derives from the name of the brother of Prometheus in Greek legend who was believed to support the heavens on his shoulders and so was often depicted holding the earth on the cover of early books containing maps of the world.

I. APHRODISIAC

The term *aphrodisiac* has been used in English since the early eighteenth century to describe anything that increases or elicits sexual desire. Derived from a similar term used in Ancient Greek, the word literally pertains to the goddess Aphrodite, who was the embodiment of love, beauty and desire in Greek myth. The mother of Eros, Aeneas and the Three Graces, Aphrodite is described as the daughter of Zeus and Dione in Homer's *Iliad*, who was said to have been born from the spray and spume of the sea near Paphos in Cyprus; her name is believed to come from the Greek word *aphros*, meaning 'foam'.

2. CALLIOPE

Patented by the American inventor Joshua C. Stoddard in Massachusetts in 1855, the *calliope* is a steam-powered organ, a musical instrument played by keyboard which operates by forcing steam through a series of pitched whistles to produce an unusually airy and strikingly loud sound. Stoddard took the name of his invention from that of the muse of epic poetry in Greek mythology, Calliope, whose name literally means 'beautiful-voiced'.

3. DAEDAL

Dating from the sixteenth century, the adjective *daedal* is a rare English word, meaning 'skilful' or 'crafty', which is derived ultimately from the same root as that of Daedalus, the name of a skilled craftsman from Greek mythology. The father of Icarus, Daedalus is known for designing and constructing the Labyrinth for the Cretan King Minos, who imprisoned the Minotaur inside. According to one story, Minos had been given a glorious white bull to sacrifice by the sea god Poseidon, but kept the bull for himself. In revenge, Poseidon conspired with Aphrodite, the goddess of desire, to have Minos's wife Pasiphaë fall in love with the creature, and ultimately give birth to the monstrous Minotaur. Horrified, Minos demanded that Daedalus create a vast maze from which the creature would never escape.

4. ECHO

According to Greek mythology, Echo was the name of a beautiful young mountain nymph who was punished by the goddess Hera for helping to conceal her husband Zeus's dalliances with the other nymphs by having her voice removed, leaving her only able to senselessly repeat the words of others. The story concludes with Echo falling in love with the handsome young Narcissus, but when he shuns her advances she flees in tears, eventually pining away into nothingness to leave only her voice behind. Her name has been used metaphorically to refer to the repetition or reverberation of a sound since the fourteenth century.

5. HERMAPHRODITE

Defined as an organism possessing both male and female sexual organs, the term *hermaphrodite* dates from the early sixteenth century in English and derives from the name of the mythological character Hermaphroditus. According to Ovid's *Metamorphoses*, Hermaphroditus was a handsome young man who was so utterly loved by the water nymph Salmacis that she longed to become entirely united with him, and so the pair were merged into a single androgynous being possessing both male and female attributes. Appropriately, even Hermaphroditus's name is a mixture of those of both his parents, Hermes and Aphrodite.

6. PHAETON

A type of four-wheeled horse-drawn carriage dating from the mid-1700s, the *phaeton* takes its name from that of the son of Clymene and Helios, the god of the sun, in Greek mythology. According to the legend, Phaeton attempted to drive his father's flaming sun-chariot across the sky but could not control it and crashed, leaving much of the earth below ablaze (although in another version of the story, Zeus kills Phaeton with a thunderbolt before he can cause any more damage). On its first appearance in the language in the late 1500s, *Phaeton* was used as another name for both a reckless or irresponsible driver and for an impetuous or destructive youth.

7. PYTHON

As the name of a type of a large tropical snake, the word *python* dates from the early 1800s in English, but as the name of a monstrous creature from Greek mythology it is found as far back as the fourteenth century. According to the myth, the Python was a huge, serpent-like dragon that presided over the oracle of Delphi. Eventually slain by the hero Apollo, the Python's remains were left to decay at Delphi in order to mark the spot where the monster had been killed – the word itself is related to the Greek word *pythein*, meaning 'to rot'.

8. SIREN

Use of the word *siren* to describe an alarm or warning sound dates from the mid-nineteenth century in English, although the term itself derives from the Sirens of Greek mythology. Famously described in Homer's *Odyssey*, the Sirens were monstrous, murderous creatures that lured sailors to their doom on the rocks around their islands with their enchanting voices and music. Often portrayed as winged, reptilian women, or else as monstrous birds with women's heads, the name *Siren* is believed to be derived from the Greek word *seira*, meaning a 'bind' or 'cord'.

9. TANTALIZE

Used since the early nineteenth century to mean to 'tease' or 'entice', the word *tantalize* in fact dates back to

141

the late sixteenth century in English when it was originally used in a less desirable sense to refer to a kind of torment in which a person would be offered or shown something that would then be taken away. The word derives from the character of Tantalus in Greek mythology who was punished for having committed a series of terrible sins: in one story, he was invited to dine with Zeus on Mount Olympus but stole the gods' food and drink and shared their secrets with his friends, whilst in another tale he murdered his son Pelops and cooked his body in a great cauldron to serve to the gods at a sacrificial feast. For his crimes, Tantalus was imprisoned in the deepest realm of the Underworld, Tartarus, where he was cursed to stand beneath a huge fruit tree surrounded by a pool of clear water, but every time he tried to take fruit from the branches or drink the water from the pool, it would be drawn back out of his reach. As well as the verb *tantalize*, Tantalus's name has also been used in English since the late 1800s to refer to a small drinks stand containing a series of bottles or decanters that, although clearly visible, are in fact locked in place.

10. TERP

A relatively uncommon term nowadays, the odd word *terp* was a popular slang term used in theatrical circles in the first half of the twentieth century. Referring to a chorus girl or professional stage dancer, the word is a shortened form of the much earlier adjective *terpsichorean*, meaning 'pertaining to dancing', which is in turn taken from the name of the Greek muse of dance, Terpsichore, whose name literally means 'enjoyment of dancing'.

XXVIII

TEN WORDS DERIVED FROM
SPORTS AND GAMES

Whilst none of the words listed here can be dated any further back than the nineteenth century in their sporting contexts, many of the names of the sports and games in which they are used are surprisingly old. Amongst the earliest of all sports recorded in English are also some of the most basic: *wrestling* was first described in the early thirteenth century, whilst *running* as a form of sport or exercise is described in Old English texts dating from as far back as the reign of Alfred the Great. *Football, archery, golf, bowling, tennis* and *racquets*, an old precursor to tennis, were all first described in the fifteenth century, with *hockey* (early 1500s), *cricket* (mid-1500s), *handball* and *billiards* (both late 1500s), *boxing* (early 1700s), *athletics* (early 1700s) and *baseball* (mid-1700s) all following on. Amongst the most recently invented of all major sports, meanwhile, are *basketball*, created by the Canadian James Naismith in 1891, and *volleyball*, or *mintonette* as it was originally known, which was invented by the American William G. Morgan in 1895.

1. ENDGAME

Today used in various contexts in English to refer to the final or concluding stage of something, the word *endgame* dates from the late nineteenth century and was originally a term from chess used to refer to the third and final decisive portion of a game (after the *opening* and *middle-game*) when a finish to the game appears imminent. Although the term is somewhat loosely defined, generally the *endgame* is said to begin when most of the pieces have been captured and removed from the board, forcing the king's movements to become more aggressive than defensive, and increasing the importance of any pawns that remain on the board.

2. FLAKY

Meaning 'crumbling' or 'disintegrating', the adjective *flaky* dates from as far back as the late 1500s in English, and is formed from the even earlier noun *flake*, which dates from the late fourteenth century. The more contemporary use of *flaky* to describe someone who is dim-witted, unreliable or eccentric (or else a combination of all three) dates from the mid-1960s, and is said to have originally been used in baseball to describe a poor-quality or underperforming player who exhibits such characteristics.

3. FLUKE

The word *fluke* has several very varied uses and meanings in English, including as the name of a type of flatfish (dating as far back as the eighth century), one of the two pronged heads of an anchor (mid-1500s), the head of a lance or spear (*c.*1600), one-half of the tail of a whale (mid-1700s), a gullible person or the victim of a crime or prank (early 1800s slang), and waste material left over from the cotton-making process (mid-1800s). In modern English, however, the word is perhaps most often encountered in the sense of a stroke of good fortune or a lucky guess, a meaning which dates from the 1850s and was originally used in billiards to refer to a successful pot

144

scored entirely by chance. In this context, the word was probably originally an English dialect term.

4. FOLLOW-THROUGH
The earliest recorded use of the word *follow-through* in English is as a verb, used in various sports – but in particular golf and cricket – to refer to the continued movement of a club or bat after the ball has been hit in order to ensure that as forceful a strike as possible is made. In this sense, the word dates from the 1890s, with use of *follow-through* as a noun recorded shortly after, and the figurative use of the term referring to the consequences or results of something dates from the 1920s.

5. JAZZ
The history of the word *jazz* is one of the most enduring mysteries of the English language, as next to nothing besides speculation is known of its origins. Helping to make the word all the more curious is the fact that in its earliest recorded use, *jazz* appears to have had no reference to music but instead seems to have been a slang term meaning something equivalent to 'enthusiasm', 'energy' or 'vigour' – the *Oxford English Dictionary* has traced the word back to an article in the sports section of the *Los Angeles Times* dated 2 April 1912 describing baseball player Ben Henderson's 'jazz curve' pitch. Given the word's apparent original meaning, of all the potential origins of *jazz* perhaps the most likely is that it is related to *jasm*, a nineteenth-century American slang term for 'pep' or 'enthusiasm', which is itself perhaps of Creole or African-American origin.

6. JINX
The word *jinx*, used to describe anything that apparently brings bad luck, dates from the early 1900s, with the first

recorded evidence of the word in English suggesting that its use in this context probably originated amongst sportsmen who would try to 'escape the jinx' if they had been playing poorly for a prolonged period of time. The word itself is believed to have developed from the much earlier seventeenth-century term *jynx*, meaning 'magic spell' or 'charm', which is itself likely rooted in the historical association of the wryneck – a bird of the woodpecker family, once widely known as the *jynx* or *yunx* – with witchcraft or black magic.

7. LINE-UP

Originally adopted from American English, the term *line-up* was first used in sporting contexts in the late 1880s to refer to the collective members of a team. The more general use of the word to refer to any assembly or assortment dates from 1904, with the first reference to a police *line-up* dating from 1907. In the 1930s the term became American criminal slang for the members of a gang involved in a heist.

8. RAINCHECK

A *raincheck* was originally a ticket given out to spectators of a baseball game that had had to be postponed due to bad weather, allowing them to return to watch a future game free of charge. Thought to have been first used in this context in the United States in the mid-1800s, the term quickly slipped into more general use and began to refer to any assurance or guarantee that a prior commitment will be fulfilled at a later date in the early twentieth century. The idiomatic phrase to *take a raincheck*, requesting that an arrangement or social meeting be postponed, dates from the 1970s.

9. SCREWBALL

A nineteenth-century term used in cricket – and later, in the 1920s, in baseball – a *screwball* was originally a type of bowl in which the bowler would apply a slight spin to the ball, giving it an erratic or surprising delivery that is intended to be difficult for the batsman to return; the word *screw* was first used in reference to such a spin in cricket in the 1840s, with the first reference to a *screwball* recorded in 1866. Implying eccentricity or abnormality, *screwball* was first used as a slang word for a madman or bizarre character in the 1930s, with the first reference to a *screwball comedy* dating from 1938.

10. STYMIE

In general use, the word *stymie* means to 'obstruct' or 'confuse', but the term was originally a specific golfing expression used to describe the blocking of a hole on the green by an opponent's ball. In this context, the word was first recorded in English in 1834 in the official rules of the Musselburgh Links golf course in East Lothian – often said to be the world's oldest continuously used golf course – in which it is explained that, 'With regard to Stimies the ball nearest the hole if within six inches shall be lifted'. The more general use of the word dates from the early 1900s.

XXIX

TEN WORDS DERIVED FROM FALCONRY

Hunting using trained birds of prey is believed to have originated in Asia more than 3,000 years ago before spreading across Europe to reach Britain sometime before the eighth to ninth century. Given this lengthy history, unsurprisingly falconry has developed a rich vocabulary all of its own – a *passenger*, for instance, is a young hawk caught in the wild and trained; a *beaching* is an old word for a small morsel of meat given to a bird to whet its appetite; and, in falconry terms, to look *eager* means to look hungry or keen to feed. Similarly, the phrases *under the thumb* and *tied around one's finger* both originally referred to the holding of a hawk's tether in the hand so that it cannot escape; to be *in a bate* or *at the bate*, meaning 'fighting' or 'panicking', refers to a frightened or impatient hawk 'bating' its wings in an attempt to escape its perch; and to be *fed up* originally referred to a bird that had eaten its fill. Ten more words that began as falconers' terms before coming to be used more generally in the language are listed here.

1. ALLURE

Both *allure* and *lure* derive from a thirteenth-century English word, *lure* or *leure*, for a piece of falconer's equipment comprising a mass of feathers or fur at the end of a long length of rope. In training the birds, falconers would customarily attach a small piece of meat to the feathered end of the lure, and once this association was learnt the promise of food would eventually be used to entice the hawks back to their owners. Originally derived from French, use of the word *lure* in English has since developed to come to mean simply an 'enticement' or 'attraction', whilst *allure* gained its initial letter from the French phrase *à lurer*, literally meaning 'to the lure'.

2. CODGER

The English colloquialism *codger*, used to describe a wizened or decrepit old man, dates from the mid-eighteenth century. Although its exact history is unclear, one suggestion claims that the word developed from a considerably older term, *cadger*, which first appeared in English in the sixteenth century as another name for an itinerant salesman or local supplier of food and other produce. Later used to describe a peddler or street-dealer, and eventually an old beggar (from where *codger* presumably derives), the word *cadger* itself literally means 'carrier', and is probably descended from an old falconer's term for a wooden frame or support, known as the *cadge*, that would have been carried by a member of a hunting party and used as a portable perch for hawks.

3. HAGGARD

Derived originally from French, the adjective *haggard* dates from the 1560s in English when it was initially used to describe an adult hawk or owl (in particular a female) that had been captured from the wild as an adult before being trained by a falconer. Figurative use of the term to describe anything or anyone equally wild or untamed developed shortly afterwards, with the eventual progression to the modern meaning of 'worn-down' or 'fatigued' first recorded in the early seventeenth century.

149

4. MEWS

Often encountered today in the addresses and names of rows of houses or cottages, the old word *mews* formerly described a row of stables or outbuildings, the term first being used for the royal stables once found at Charing Cross in central London. Dating from the turn of the fourteenth to fifteenth century, these original *mews* in turn took their name from the even earlier falconers' *mews* which once stood on the same site – derived from the French phrase *en mue*, a *mew* was originally a small cage or enclosure used in falconry, in which a bird was placed during moulting.

5. MUSKET

On its first appearance in the English language in the fourteenth century, the word *musket* was originally used as a name for the male sparrowhawk. In this sense, the term is presumably based on an Old French word for a fly, *musche*, with the addition of the suffix *-et* (used to form diminutives, as in *maisonette* and *kitchenette*) presumably alluding to the fact that the male sparrowhawk is much smaller than the female. Quite how the bird's name came to be used as that for a type of firearm is unclear, but it seems apparent that by the sixteenth century *musket* had come to be used as another name for the bolt fired from a crossbow – perhaps intended to imply some sense of the speed or accuracy of a hunting hawk, the word's eventual association with weaponry seems to have stemmed from there.

6. POLTROON

Used since the early sixteenth century in English as another name for a mean-spirited coward or con-temptible fool, *poltroon* was also once used in falconry to describe a bird whose talons had been clipped or removed to prevent it from damaging its catch too badly. The word is descended, via French and Italian, from the Latin word for a young animal, *pullus*, from which the verb *pullulate*, meaning to 'birth' or 'bring forth', is similarly derived. Its use in falconry, however, is thought to be descended from a Latin phrase, *pollice truncus*, literally meaning 'maimed in the thumb', which was originally used of soldiers who shirked military service by deliberately injuring themselves.

7. POUNCE

Use of the verb *pounce* to mean to 'seize upon' or to 'ambush' dates from the mid-seventeenth century in English, and originally described the action of a bird of prey swooping down upon and catching something in its talons, a sense developed from an earlier and now obsolete use of the word to describe the innermost claw of a falcon. More recent figurative senses of the word meaning to 'spring into action' or 'notice suddenly' were both first recorded in the mid-1800s.

8. PRIDE

Use of the word *pride* to mean the 'best' or 'highest' of something – the sense employed when something is described as being *the pride of* – dates from the mid-fifteenth century and is a direct development from the Old English-origin adjective *proud*. Saying that something is in *pride of place*, however, is a Shakespearean coinage referring to the highest point in the flight of a hunting bird of prey, from where it swoops down on to its target. The phrase is first attested in English in *Macbeth* (II. iv), in which Shakespeare describes 'a falcon towering in her pride of place'.

9. ROUSE

Thought to have been adopted into the language from French, the word *rouse* was first recorded in English in the late fifteenth century, when it was initially used as a falconer's term for a bird shaking or fluffing up its feathers. Later used in hunting to apply to the action of scaring game birds from the undergrowth, extended use of the word to mean 'provoke' or 'disturb' dates from the mid-1500s in the language, with the derivative *arouse*, meaning to 'stir from sleep' or 'awaken', first attested in Shakespeare's *Henry VI, Part 2* (IV. i).

10. TURN-TAIL

Used to describe a coward or deserter, or else someone who goes back on their principles, the word *turn-tail* derives from the old phrase to 'turn tail' meaning to 'abandon' or 'defy', which was originally used to describe falcons and other birds that would be said to 'turn tail' when fleeing from danger. Use of the word as a verb in this sense was first recorded in English in late sixteenth century, with the noun *turn-tail* developing in the early 1600s.

XXX

TEN WORDS DERIVED FROM HORSES

The word *horse* ranks amongst the oldest recorded words in the entire English language, is statistically the most frequently used animal name in written English, and is recorded in more than sixty different senses and 700 different derivatives and phrases in the *Oxford English Dictionary*. Besides familiar expressions like *straight from the horse's mouth* (thought to have originally referred to helpful betting tips) and *flogging a dead horse*, the word appears in a great many more curious English terms and expressions including *talk horse*, meaning 'boast'; *go on a horse with ten toes*, meaning simply 'go on foot'; *horse-neck*, a drink of ginger ale mixed with a spirit and flavoured with lemon; *ride a horse that was foaled of an acorn*, a seventeenth-century euphemism for being hanged; *half-horse half-alligator*, a nineteenth-century nickname for Mississippi boatmen, who supposedly exhibited the strength and skills of both animals; and the *horse latitudes*, two subtropical bands of relatively calm air, lying roughly 30–35 degrees north and south of the equator. Quite where this last expression comes from is debatable, but one folk etymology claims that the calm air found in these regions would often lead ships heading from Europe to the Americas to become trapped for days on end, and with supplies dwindling on board, any horses being transported across the Atlantic would typically either die of dehydration or be slaughtered and eaten by the crew.

1. BIDET

The word *bidet*, as well as being the name of a bathroom fixture, is actually the French word for 'pony' (derived from the verb *bider*, meaning 'to trot'), and indeed the word's earliest recorded use in English is as another name for a small horse. Quite why the household *bidet* was given this name is unclear, but it has been suggested that the French furniture-makers who first began manufacturing them in the sixteenth century used the name as a playful reference to the fact that the *bidet* is straddled in the same way as a horse.

2. BOGGLE

Use of the word *boggle* to mean to 'confuse' or 'amaze', dates from the early nineteenth century, with the first reference to the phrase *the mind boggles* dated 1899. Before this, the word was used in various different senses in English, including to 'fumble' or 'handle clumsily' (eighteenth century); to 'quibble' or 'hesitate' (seventeenth century); to 'startle', 'take alarm' or, in its earliest sense, 'shy', like a startled horse (sixteenth century). This original sense of the word – found in the old phrase to *take boggle*, meaning 'take fright' – is said to be derived from the earlier sixteenth-century English word *bogle*, which referred to a type of spectre that was said to be seen by horses when they suddenly reared up.

3. CAVALCADE

The word *cavalcade* was adopted into English from French and is derived via the Latin verb *caballicare*, meaning 'to ride on horseback', from *caballus*, an old-fashioned and chiefly poetic Latin word for 'horse', from which the related terms *cavalier* and *cavalry* are also derived. On its first appearance in the language in the sixteenth century, *cavalcade* was originally used to refer simply to any horseback ride or march, and then to a mounted procession or convoy of horseback riders, before its meaning eventually broadened to the more modern senses of a 'parade' or 'pageant', or else a 'series' or 'sequence of events'. Most recently of all, however, *cavalcade* gave rise to the suffix *-cade* in the early twentieth century, from which the Americanisms *motorcade* (1911), *autocade* (1922) and *aquacade* (1937) have since all been derived.

4. CHIVALRY

Meaning 'courteous or gallant behaviour', the word *chivalry* dates back as far as the thirteenth century in English. Adopted into the language from an old equivalent French term *chevalerie* (which is in turn descended from the Latin word for 'horseman', *caballarius*), at its very earliest the word was used to refer collectively to mounted knights or men-at-arms, or else to a body of armed forces as a whole. It was the courageous, gallant behaviour and prowess of these knights which ultimately influenced the word's meaning today.

5. CROUPIER

In modern English, the word *croupier* is usually used to refer to the attendant of a gambling table, whose job it is to collect and pay bets, deal cards and assist in the running of the game. In this context, the word dates from as far back as the early 1700s, but previously it was used to refer to a gambler's associate or 'second' who would aid him throughout the game by backing or going half on his bets, or by offering advice or even extra cash. It is this meaning of the word, now largely obsolete in English, which is descended from the word's original meaning in its native French, wherein a *croupier* was a person who would ride behind another on the rump or *croup* of a horse.

6. HENCHMAN

The word *henchman* dates back to the fourteenth century in English, when it was originally used to refer to a squire who would have ridden alongside a nobleman during processions or parades. The word itself is derived from the Old English term *hengest*, meaning 'horse' or 'stallion', and so a *hengestman* (of which *henchman* is a simplified form) was literally a 'horseman'. The word largely dropped out of use in English in the 1600s, but was revived in the more general sense of a 'follower' or 'supporter' in the mid-nineteenth century.

7. HIPPOCAMPUS

Hippocampus is derived via Latin from the Ancient Greek words *hippos*, meaning 'horse', and *kampos*, meaning 'sea monster'. In fact the word was originally used as the name of a legendary sea creature having the head and forelegs of a horse and the body and tail of a dolphin or fish, which typically was depicted pulling the chariot of the Greek god of the sea, Poseidon. Based on this mythological description, on its first appearance in English in the late 1500s the word was used as another name for the seahorse, and in fact the genus to which all known species of seahorse now belong is still named *Hippocampus*. Today, the word is probably most well known as the term for a part of the brain – one of two symmetrically-located regions now known to be crucial to memory, spatial awareness and navigation – which was given its name in the early 1700s due to its supposed resemblance to a seahorse.

8. TRAPPINGS

Generally meaning 'equipment' or 'superficial possessions', the word *trappings* dates from the late sixteenth century in English. At its earliest, however, the word dates back as far as the 1300s, when a *trapping* was originally an ornamental cover or blanket spread over the back and saddle of a horse. Also known simply as a *trap* or a *trapper* (and later all but replaced by the equivalent French word *caparison*), the term is ultimately descended via French from the Latin word *drappus*, meaning 'cloth' or 'drape'.

9. JAUNT

As a verb, the word *jaunt* dates from the late sixteenth century in English when it was originally used to mean 'ride a horse back and forth', often with the intention of tiring it out. In this context, the origin of the word is unclear but is perhaps a derivative of either the similar term *jaunce*, meaning to 'make a horse prance up and down', or the earlier *jounce*, meaning to 'bump' or 'move joltingly', both of which are presumed to be of French origin. The more modern sense of the verb *jaunt*, meaning to 'take a trip', dates from the mid-1600s, whilst the noun *jaunt* first appeared in the late 1500s in reference to an exhausting journey, before being first used simply of any voyage or excursion in the 1670s.

10. TACKY

Use of the word *tacky* to mean 'sticky' or 'adhesive' dates from the late eighteenth century in English and is derived from *tack*, a much earlier word dating from the Middle English period that referred to anything used to join two things together. Use of *tacky* to mean 'tasteless' or 'shabby', however, is believed to have originated in the United States in the early nineteenth century when the word referred to any small, cheap or second-rate horse. Quite how the word came to be used in this context is unknown.

XXXI

TEN WORDS DERIVED FROM ANIMALS

Animals' names are common not only in the origins of ordinary words – in which case they often refer either to the shape of something (as in PLYCHON) or to its character (as in CALLET) – but also in the origins of proper nouns, including first names like *Philip*, adapted from the Greek *Philippos*, meaning 'lover of horses'; *Bernard* and *Bernadette*, descended from the Norse word for 'bear', *bera*; and names like *Leon*, *Lionel* and *Leonard*, all of which are forms of the Latin word for 'lion', *leo*. Place names too often make reference to animals, with examples found all over the world: *Oxford* would originally have referred to a fording point on a river where oxen could cross; the capital of Switzerland, *Bern*, is said to be named from the German for 'bear', *bär*; *Panama* is said to mean literally 'an abundance of fish' in a local native language; and *Singapore* takes its name from a Malay word meaning 'lion city'. Slightly more unusual examples, however, include the Ghanaian capital *Accra*, whose name literally means 'ants' on account of the vast number of anthills in the area, and *Khartoum*, the capital of Sudan, whose name is derived from an Arabic word meaning 'the end of the elephant's trunk', referring to the city's position on a narrow strip of land formed by the confluence of the Blue and White Niles.

1. ANTIPELARGY

The obscure seventeenth-century word *antipelargy* means a 'mutual love or kindness', especially in reference to the reciprocal love between a child and its parents, or to a child's love and care for its parents in their old age. Adapted into English from an earlier equivalent French term, the word is ultimately derived from the Ancient Greek for stork, *pelargos*, as storks were once considered to be particularly affectionate to their young.

2. ARCTIC

The word *arctic* is derived from the Greek word *arktos*, meaning 'bear'. Despite popular belief, this meaning does not refer to the polar bears living in the far north of Europe, but rather to the prominent position of the constellation *Ursa Major*, 'The Great Bear', in the northern sky. Ultimately, on its first appearance in English in the fourteenth century, the word *arctic* was used as an adjective to refer to the celestial North Pole, and it was not until the mid-sixteenth century that the word came to be used to describe the northernmost region of the earth.

3. CALLET

The English insult *callet* or *callat* dates from the sixteenth century. Used several times by Shakespeare, the word describes either a lewd or lasciviously brazen woman ('a beggar in his drink / Could not have laid such terms upon his callat', *Othello*, IV. ii), or else a nagging old scold or carp ('A callat / Of boundless tongue, who late hath beat her husband / And now baits me!', *The Winter's Tale*, II. iii). Either way, the word is thought to be derived from an Old French word for a fool, *caillette*, which is itself a diminutive of the French word for the quail, *caille*, a tiny game bird that has long been regarded as a supposedly foolish creature.

4. CANOPY

Canopy was borrowed into the English language from French in the fourteenth century. In the sense of a thin, protective covering, the word is descended via the Latin *conopeum* from the Ancient Greek word for a mosquito net or a covered chair, *konopeion*, which is in turn a derivative of the Greek word for 'mosquito' or 'gnat', *konops*. The French culinary term *canapé* is of identical origin, but was originally the name of a type of couch fitted with a thin canopy known as a bandaquin – the fillings of a *canapé* were said to sit atop a layer of pastry in the same way as a person would sit upon a couch.

5. CHOUETTE

Chouette is the French name for the barn owl, and has been used in English since the late nineteenth century as the name of a form of play in certain games – most notably backgammon, but also some card games like bezique and gin rummy – in which one player competes against all of the other players together, who must effectively work as a team in order to win. The term derives from an earlier French expression *faire la chouette*, which was used more generally to refer to several players of any game turning against a single player all at once. It is likely that the phrase pertains to the fact that like many other birds of prey, barn owls are often mobbed by gangs of smaller birds when they believe it poses a threat.

6. DELPHINIUM

A popular family of flowering plants, typically with tall spikes of blue or purple flowers, the name *delphinium* is of Latin origin but is based on the Ancient Greek word *delphis*, meaning 'dolphin'. So called as the nectar-bearing parts of the flower heads are said to resemble dolphins, the *delphinium* was given its name by the noted Swedish botanist and zoologist Carl Linnaeus in the mid-eighteenth century.

7. PLYCHON

The *plychon* is the name of an early dentist's tool thought to have been used to extract teeth. First recorded in the seventeenth century, the word *plychon* likely derives from a misinterpretation or corruption of *pelican*, which besides being the name of a seabird was once also the name of a kind of two-pronged and hinged surgical tool, presumably named in reference to its shape. Both *plychon* and, in this sense at least, *pelican* have long since dropped out of use in English, as thankfully have the tools that they describe.

8. STURDY

In its earliest use in English dating back to the early 1200s, the word *sturdy* variously meant 'brave', 'reckless' or 'furious', and it was not until the late fourteenth century that it came to be used to mean 'strong' or 'robust'. The word is presumed to be of French origin and is likely based on an old-fashioned word, *estourdi*, meaning 'stunned' or 'dazed', which is in turn descended from the Latin word for the thrush, *turdus*. Quite where this association comes from is unclear, yet *as drunk as a thrush* was once a popular saying in France.

9. TRAGEDY

Perhaps one of the strangest animal-related etymologies in the whole of the English language, the word *tragedy* derives via French and Latin from a Greek word, *tragodia*, literally meaning 'goat-song'. Precisely why Ancient Greek *tragedies* were given this name is unknown, although one suggestion claims that the word perhaps refers to actors dressing in goatskins and other animal furs so as to portray the satyrs and other mythical beings that often appeared in the stories.

10. URCHIN

Since it was first recorded in the English language in the late thirteenth century, the word *urchin* has come to be used to describe a variety of different things, including a hunchback (early 1500s); a badly behaved child (mid-1500s); a goblin or elf (late 1500s); a demon (late 1500s); an ugly, ill-tempered woman or hag (1500s-1600s); a sea urchin (1600s); and part of an engine (mid-1800s). In its earliest use, however, an *urchin* was actually a hedgehog and the word itself is believed to be derived from the creature's Latin name, *ericius*.

XXXII

TEN WORDS DERIVED FROM ROCKS AND STONES

Besides the ten entries listed here, the words *rock* and *stone* have each provided the English language with a vast number of words and expressions in their own right, many of which are considerably older than they might appear. To *leave no stone unturned*, for instance, dates from the sixteenth century; to be *as steady* or *as solid as a rock* dates from the seventeenth century; and to be within *a stone's throw* dates from the eighteenth century. To be *on the rocks*, meaning 'short of cash', meanwhile, has been used since the late 1800s, although in reference to an alcoholic drink served over ice it dates from the early 1900s, as do *between a rock and a hard place*, *rock paper scissors* (or *scissors paper stone*), and *rock and roll*, which was first used in the lyrics to a popular song, 'Rock It for Me', written by American songwriters Kay and Sue Werner in 1938.

1. CALCULUS
Both the Latin word *calx*, meaning 'lime' or 'stone', and its earlier Ancient Greek equivalent *khalix*, meaning 'pebble', are the origin of a surprising number of English words including *chalk*, *calcify*, both *calculate* and *calculator*, and *calculus*. First recorded in English in the seventeenth century, the word *calculus* literally means 'little stone' in Latin, and gave its name to a branch of mathematics as

such stones would once have been used as aids in counting and reckoning sums. This literal sense of the word, incidentally, is maintained in medicine wherein a *calculus* is another name for a stone that forms naturally in the kidney or other organs of the body.

2. CLOUD

Surprisingly, the Old English word *clud*, from which the Modern English *cloud* is derived, was originally used to mean a 'mass of rock', 'boulder' or 'hill', and is related to a handful of similar words like *clod* and *clot*. This meaning was first recorded in the language in the ninth century, yet appears to have fallen out of use in the Middle English period when, from the early fourteenth century onwards, *cloud* adopted its modern meaning. It is presumed that the similarity between dense grey rainclouds and large rocks or stones is what instigated the alteration from one meaning to the other, whilst the Old English word for 'cloud' that *clud* replaced, *wolcen*, is today retained in *welkin*, an old-fashioned or poetic term for the sky or heavens.

3. CROMLECH

A *cromlech* is an ancient megalithic structure or monument, often (in Britain and Ireland, at least) in the form of an underground tomb marked by a large stack of flat stone slabs above the ground. Also known as a *dolmen* (a name believed to be of Celtic origin, essentially meaning 'table-stones'), in northern France and other parts of the continent where similar monuments are found, the word *cromlech* can also be used to refer to a stone circle. Either way, the term is derived from the Welsh words *crom*, meaning 'arched' or 'crooked', and *llech*, meaning 'flat stone'.

4. DILAPIDATED

Meaning 'run down' or 'ruined', the adjective *dilapidated* dates from the early nineteenth century in English, and is derived from the earlier if less commonly used sixteenth-century verb *dilapidate*, meaning to 'bring to ruin' or 'decay'. The root of both words is the Latin verb *dilapidare*, which meant literally 'to scatter like stones' and is ultimately derived from the Latin word for 'stone' or 'rock', *lapis*, from which gemstone *lapis lazuli* (literally 'azure stone') also takes its name. Of similar origin is the old seventeenth-century verb *lapidate*, which as well as meaning simply to 'throw stones' was once also used more specifically to mean 'stone to death'.

5. LITHIUM

Chemical element number 3, *lithium* (Li) is a soft, silvery-white alkali metal, typically considered both the lightest of all metals and the least dense of all of the elements that are solid at room temperature; one cubic-centimetre of *lithium* would weigh just 0.53 g (0.02 oz). Its discovery is credited to the eighteenth- to nineteenth-century Swedish chemist Johan August Arfwedson, who detected what he believed was a new element in a sample of the mineral petalite in 1817. Although he failed to isolate it (a feat achieved four years later by the English chemist William Thomas Brande), Arfwedson and his mentor Jöns Berzelius nevertheless named their discovery *lithia*, derived from the Greek word for 'stone', *lithos*, referring to the fact that it had been identified amidst a solid substance. Two other elements also take their name from 'stones', namely *calcium* (Ca), derived at length from the Latin *calx*, and *tungsten* (W), whose name literally means 'heavy stone' in Swedish.

6. PARSLEY

The word *parsley* is believed to be a blend of two of the herb's earlier English names, namely *petersilie*, of Latin origin, and *persile*, adopted from French. At its very earliest, however, *parsley* is descended from the Greek *petroselinon*, a name literally meaning 'rock celery' and derived in turn from the Greek word for 'rock', *petros*. This same Greek root is also the origin of words like *saltpetre, petroleum, petrify* and the name *Peter*.

7. ROCOCO

Used as the name of an elaborate eighteenth-century French style of baroque art and architecture – and hence, adjectivally, referring to anything ornately old-fashioned or complicated – the word *rococo* was first used in English in the early 1800s. Derived directly from French, the term is believed to be based on the earlier French term *rocaille*, a form of decoration or ornamentation made from shells, beads or small stones, which is itself taken from the French word for 'rock', *roche*.

8. SAXIFRAGE

First recorded in English in the mid-fifteenth century, *saxifrage* is a type of low-lying flowering plant found predominantly in alpine or sub-Arctic areas that is today popular as a bedding plant in rockeries and in regions with poor soil. Derived via French from the Latin *saxifragus*, the plant's name literally means 'stone-breaking' (from the Latin *saxum*, 'stone', and the verb *frangere*, meaning 'to shatter' or 'to break') presumably referring both to its habit of growing out of clefts in rocks and stones, and to the traditional idea that *saxifrage* can be used medicinally to break up kidney stones and other similar deposits in the body. The same derivation is the origin of the word *saxifragine*, the name of a type of nineteenth-century gunpowder.

9. SCRUPULOUS

Today generally taken to mean simply 'conscientious' or 'meticulous', the modern use of the word *scrupulous* is a slightly diluted version of its original meaning, dating from the sixteenth century, which instead implied an overly fastidious and self-doubting obsession with matters of right or wrong. The word is based around the much earlier term *scruple* (still used today to denote a qualm or moral misgiving), a derivative of the Latin *scrupulus*, a 'small sharp stone', which was used figuratively by the Roman scholar and philosopher Cicero to imply something that causes concern or anxiety in the sense of having a stone in one's shoe.

10. STEIN

As the name of a type of large, earthenware drinking-vessel usually used to hold beer or ale, the word *stein* was first recorded in English in the mid-nineteenth century. Adopted from German, the word is actually a shortened form of *Steinkrug*, literally meaning 'stone jug'. The German *stein* is also found in English in the names of several different types of rocks and minerals including *mandelstein* ('almond-stone') and *schaalstein* ('skin-stone'), and in an alternative name of the Alpine ibex, *steinbock*, whose name translates literally as 'stone buck'.

XXXIII

TEN WORDS DERIVED FROM WATERWAYS

Listed here are ten words derived from some root form referring to some form of watercourse or waterway, such as a river, sea, stream or lake. Words designating geographical features like these tend to be particularly old due to the obvious need for humans to describe the world around us. *Sea, mere, brook, stream, burn, tide, ford* and *well*, for instance, were all found in Old English and are more than 1,000 years old. *Ocean* is a more recent addition to the language adopted from French in the late thirteenth century and descended ultimately from the Greek word *okeanos*, which referred to the vast river that the Ancient Greeks supposed encircled the world. The word *river* was also adopted from French in the early fourteenth century and replaced the Old English word *ea*, which is still retained in some dialects of English and in English place names like Eton, Mersey and Romney.

1. ARCHIPELAGO
The word *archipelago* was first recorded in English in the early 1500s, when it was originally used as another name for the Aegean Sea, the body of water lying between mainland Greece and Turkey. The word literally means 'chief sea' in Greek, formed from the prefix *arkhi-* (the same prefix seen in words like *archduke* and *archbishop*) and *pelagos*, the Greek word for 'sea'. As the Aegean is so

169

famously strewn with islands, eventually *archipelago* came to apply less specifically to any body of water containing a vast number of islands and eventually, in the nineteenth century, to a group or chain of islands itself.

2. BARBICAN

Today, the word *barbican* is probably most familiar to English speakers thanks to the names of various performing arts facilities and theatres, most notably the famous Barbican Centre in London, whilst the original meaning of the word has been all but lost. Historically, a *barbican* was an outer tower or gatehouse at the entrance to a castle, but the word could also be used to describe a fort or similar defensive structure at the end of a bridge, a temporary or movable wooden watchtower, and a narrow opening or loophole in the wall of a fort through which arrows or guns could be fired. Dating from the fourteenth century in English, the word itself is believed to have been adapted from the equivalent French term *barbacane* or *barbaquenne*, which in turn is a derivative of the Arabic word for a canal or water channel, *barbakh*.

3. DEBACLE

Used in a general sense to describe a calamitous disaster or fiasco, the word *debacle* was originally a French geographical term, *débâcle* (from the verb *débâcler*, meaning 'to free' or 'to unbar'), used to describe the melting of river ice during the spring thaw and the sudden flood or surge of water that ensues. The word was first recorded in this original sense in English in the early 1800s, whilst the first use of the word in the metaphorical sense of a sudden downfall or disaster was first recorded in William Makepeace Thackeray's novel *Vanity Fair* in 1847.

4. DERIVE

On its earliest appearance in English in the late fifteenth century, the verb *derive* originally meant to draw or divert water from one location to another, particularly in the sense of channelling water from its source into a stream or reservoir. In this sense, the word is descended from the Latin equivalent verb *derivare*, which is itself formed from the Latin word for a stream or brook, *rivus*. Its more general sense, meaning to 'originate' or 'develop', did not begin to appear until the mid-sixteenth century, with the first use of *derive* in an etymological context first used in 1567.

5. FAIRWAY

As a golf term, referring to the main length of a golf course between the tee and the green, the word *fairway* dates from the early 1910s. Originally, however, the word was used to describe a navigable river channel or waterway, especially one deep enough for larger boats and vessels to be piloted down, or else one acting as a route between sandbanks or similar obstacles down which a ship can be transported into and out of harbour safely. Dating from the sixteenth century, it is this sense of an open, unobstructed area between surrounding hazards or more treacherous terrain that is maintained in the use of *fairway* in golf.

6. LACUNA

First used as an English word in the mid-seventeenth century, the term *lacuna* appears in a variety of different contexts in the language, all of which imply some sense of an empty space or hollow – at its very earliest, in the mid-1600s, the word was used to refer to a missing or intentionally blank section in a document. Now, a *lacuna* can also be a microscopic space between two neighbour-ing cells; a cavity in a bone; a sac or space in the anatomy of certain creatures, used in their circulatory system; a tiny indentation or pit in the surface of a leaf; or, in lin-guistics, the 'gap' found when a word from one language has no obvious translation in another. Also used more generally as another word for a pit or hole, *lacuna* is of Latin origin and is ultimately derived from the Latin for 'lake', *lacus*.

7. MAELSTROM
In its earliest form, dating from in the late sixteenth cen-tury in English, the word *maelstrom* is believed to have specifically applied to a vast and devastatingly powerful whirlpool located off the Arctic coast of Norway that was capable of drawing in ships and other vessels from a con-siderable distance and pulling them beneath the waves. A loanword from Dutch, the word is derived from the verb *malen*, meaning 'to whirl' or 'to grind', and *stroom*, the Dutch word for 'stream'. The metaphorical use of the word, referring to a tumultuous state of confusion or chaos, dates from the nineteenth century.

8. RHEUM
Rheum is the general name for any of the thin, watery fluids naturally secreted by the body, and in particular those discharged from the eyes, nose or mouth. Produced by the mucus membranes of the head, *rheum* was once thought to be produced in the brain and was even believed to be capable of causing disease, although both theories are now known to be untrue. The word itself entered the language in the fourteenth century from an equivalent French term *reume*, which is in turn derived from the Greek word for a stream, *rheuma*, and ultimately

the verb *rhein*, meaning 'to flow'. The same root is the source of several other English words, including the similar term *catarrh* (taken from the Greek *katarreo*, meaning 'flow down'), *rheostat*, *rheumatoid*, and the medical suffix *-rrhoea*.

9. RIVAL

The earliest recorded use of the word *rival* in English dates from the fifteenth century when, far from its familiar modern meaning, the word described a shore or riverbank suitable for landing a boat. The sense of the word to mean 'competitor' or 'opponent' dates from considerably later, towards the end of the sixteenth century, and stems from the related Latin word *rivalis* (a derivative of *rivus*, meaning 'stream'), which was historically used to describe a person who lives on the opposite side of a river from another with whom they compete over use of the water.

10. ROSEMARY

The fragrant Mediterranean herb *rosemary* was originally known as *rosmarine*, a name dating back into antiquity and first used in the early Old English period. This historical name, seldom used in English today, is derived directly from the Latin phrase *ros marinus* meaning literally 'dew of the sea' (from the Latin *mare*, meaning 'sea', as in *maritime* and *submarine*), indicating that the plant typically requires very little water and can in some areas survive solely on the water it obtains from nearby sea mists and frets. The corrupted name *rosemary* first appeared in the early 1400s.

XXXIV

TEN WORDS DERIVED FROM
THE HUMAN BODY

Words derived from the names of parts of the human body are actually quite numerous in English and besides the ten listed here, those derived from 'head', 'heart', 'hand' and 'foot' are all discussed in their own chapters elsewhere. English contains a similarly large number of phrases and expressions that contain some kind of reference to the body, perhaps the oldest of which is to *hold your tongue*, which dates back as far as the ninth century. To *put words in someone's mouth*, meanwhile, dates from the fourteenth century, whilst to keep something *at arm's length*, to *find your legs*, to *not have a leg to stand on*, to *fight tooth and nail*, to *have your back against the wall*, to *cut your own throat*, to *have your heart in your mouth*, and to do something *heart in hand* all date from the sixteenth century. Many expressions like these, however, have long since dropped out of common use in the language – to *put out someone's eyes with gifts*, for instance, was an Elizabethan expression meaning to 'bribe', whilst the old phrase to *talk* or *fish out the bottom of your stomach*, meaning to divulge your closest secrets or thoughts, dates from the 1530s.

I. ACCOLADE
The word *accolade* dates from the early seventeenth century, when it originally applied only to the bestowal of a

knighthood – the word did not gain its more general use for a prize or an award of privilege until the mid-nineteenth century. The word is derived from the Old French *accoler*, meaning 'to embrace around the neck', referring to the action of embracing or resting a sword on the shoulders in order to confer a knighthood, which is in turn derived from the French *col*, meaning 'neck', and the Latin word *collum*, as in *collar*. The rare word *accoll*, meaning to 'embrace' or 'throw your arms around someone's neck', is of similar origin.

2. DATE

In English, the use of the word *date* as the name of the fruit of the date palm dates from the early 1300s, and precedes the use of the word to mean a 'period of time' by almost a century. Although both words were adopted into the language from French, the edible *date* derives its name at length from the Latin *dactylus* and Greek *daktylos*, meaning 'finger', presumably hinting either at its shape or to the shape of the palm's leaves. The word *date* in reference to time, alternatively, comes from the Latin word *datum*, meaning 'given', and developed from the Ancient Roman practice of marking official letters and documents with the precise place and time at which they were 'given' to messengers for delivery.

3. GARGOYLE

The word *gargoyle* was first recorded in English in the fourteenth century, describing the intentionally grotesque stone figures of animals or monsters that serve as waterspouts, channelling rainwater from the gutters and away from the walls below. It is thought that the word *gargoyle* is derived from an Old French term literally meaning 'throat', *gargouille*, as the water is typically channelled out of the *gargoyles'* mouths. The word *gargle* is of similar origin, as is *gargil*, an old name for the gullet, and *gargolette*, a large pot or vessel used to cool water.

4. GENUINE

In its earliest sense, dating from the sixteenth century, the word *genuine* was used to describe anything natural or native, as opposed to foreign or acquired; its later generalized use, for anything real or non-counterfeit, dates from the mid-1600s. The word is presumed to have its origins in the Latin verb *gignere*, meaning 'to give birth to' or 'to beget', but it is likely that it was at some point also influenced by the Latin word for 'knee', *genu*, supposedly referring to an ancient custom wherein a father would acknowledge the paternity of a newborn baby by sitting it on his knee.

5. GLOSSARY

First recorded in English in the fourteenth century, the literal meaning of the word *glossary* is simply a 'collection of glosses', short explanatory comments or translations of obscure or foreign words that were historically written in the margin or between the lines of a text in order to clarify its content. These *glosses* in turn derive their name via Latin from the Ancient Greek word *glossa* or *glotta* (as in *epiglottis* and *polyglot*) meaning 'language' or, literally, 'tongue'.

6. HYSTERIA

The word *hysteria* was coined for use in a medical journal in 1801, contrived from the earlier seventeenth-century medical adjective *hysterical*, which is in turn descended from the Greek word for the womb, *hystera*. Hysterical symptoms were once inaccurately only associated with women, and so were presumed to be brought on by some kind of condition of the uterus. This misconception began in Ancient Greece – Plato and his fellow scholars believed that the womb was a living being, capable of moving around a woman's body – and lasted well into the nineteenth century until experiments by the French neurologist Jean-Martin Charcot, and later Sigmund Freud, began to establish *hysteria* as a purely psychological condition.

7. HYPOCHONDRIA

Dating from the sixteenth century, the word *hypochondria* is primarily an anatomical term used to refer to the two regions of the upper abdomen, left and right, lying above the stomach and beneath the ribs. The word itself literally means 'beneath the cartilage', as each *hypochondrium* contains the organs that lie beneath the cartilage of the chest and breastbone. The connection between this region of the body and the more familiar use of the word, properly known as *hypochondriasis*, to describe a morbid obsession with ill health stems from the historical belief that maladies of these organs of the upper body were the cause of all feelings of melancholy and unease.

8. RECALCITRANT

Meaning 'obstinate and uncooperative' or 'disobedient', the adjective *recalcitrant* originally entered into English as a French loanword in the late eighteenth century. The term is descended from the Latin verb *recalcitrare*, meaning literally 'to kick back' like a horse, which is itself based on the Latin word for 'heel', *calx*.

9. SUPERCILIOUS

Describing someone haughty or pompously disdainful, the adjective *supercilious* entered the English language directly from Latin in the sixteenth century. It is a derivative of the Latin word *supercilium*, which, although also used to mean 'haughtiness' or 'arrogance', is in fact the Latin word for 'eyebrow'. Comprised of the Latin prefix *super-*, meaning 'above', and *cilium*, meaning 'eyelid', the term implies that a *supercilious* person's expressions of contempt would be made by simply raising an eyebrow.

10. TERGIVERSATE

Variously used to mean 'desert', 'evade', 'dither' or 'retreat', the somewhat obscure verb *tergiversate* was first recorded in English in the late seventeenth century, derived from the earlier and equally diverse noun *tergiversation*, meaning the 'abandonment of a cause', 'act of changing sides' or 'deliberate evasion of a point'. The word is derived from the Latin verb *tergiversare*, literally meaning 'to turn one's back', which is itself based on the Latin name for the back, *tergum.*

XXXV

TEN WORDS DERIVED FROM MEDICINE

Whilst many medical terms tend to be fairly complex and are typically derived from classical Latin and Greek roots, the ten words listed here were all first used in medical contexts before gaining wider and more general use elsewhere in the language, and include such familiar terms as DRASTIC, RECIPE and REFRIGERATE. Oppositely, English also contains a number of terms that are now almost exclusively used in medicine yet were originally used elsewhere. For instance, on its first appearance in the language in the early fourteenth century, the word *doctor* was used to describe a religious scholar or philosopher, and is descended from the Latin verb *docere*, meaning 'to teach'. Similarly, a *nurse* was originally a woman who looked after or fostered children (a meaning retained in the word *nursery* and the phrase *wet nurse*), whilst *hospital* was originally another name for a guesthouse and is derived from the same root – Latin *hospitale*, meaning a 'place for guests' – as the word *hospitality*.

I. ABBREVIATION

The word *abbreviation* was adopted into English from French in the fifteenth century, and is ultimately descended from the same Latin root – *breviare*, meaning 'to shorten' – as similar words like *brief, brevity* and *abridge*. The earliest record of the word comes from the *Chirurgia Magna* (*The Great Surgery*), a work by the fourteenth-century French physician Guy de Chauliac, first translated into English in the 1420s. In this context, *abbreviation* was originally used to refer to the reduction in size or contraction of a muscle or similar part of the body; it was not until the late 1500s that the word was first used for a shortened word or phrase. Of comparable history is *relaxation*, which de Chauliac first used to describe the loosening or softening of a part of the body or else the release of tension in a muscle, and it was not until the mid-1500s that the term came to refer to a period of rest or leisure.

2. ATTRACTION

Adopted into the language from French and ultimately descended from Latin, the word *attraction* dates back to the early sixteenth century in English when it was originally a medical term used variously to refer to the inhalation of breath, the absorption or intake of food or similar matter by the body, or the drawing out of infection or diseased fluids from the body. A more general sense of the word developed in the early seventeenth century, with the first scientific reference to magnetic *attraction* found in the works of Francis Bacon in the 1620s. In the sense of something that draws a crowd, meanwhile, an *attraction* dates from the early 1800s.

3. CATHARSIS

Derived from the Greek word *katharsis*, meaning 'purging' or 'cleansing', *catharsis* first entered the language in the early nineteenth century, whilst the adjective *cathartic*, meaning 'satisfying' or 'cleansing', dates back to the mid-seventeenth century. Both forms of the word were originally used only in medical contexts and related fairly unpleasantly to any physical purging or evacuation of the body, such as vomiting or emptying the bowels. Over time, the use of both terms broadened to come to imply simply a cleansing or purifying release of emotion, with the first reference to psychological *catharsis* dating in English from 1909.

4. DRASTIC

Derived at length from the Greek word *drastikos*, meaning 'effective' or 'active', the first use of the word *drastic* in English was in reference to a medical treatment that was especially strong or potent, and in particular one that was intended to have a strong purgative effect on the digestive system. Dating from the seventeenth century, this medical use of the word largely dropped away in the nineteenth century, when the more general sense of *drastic*, meaning simply 'extreme' or 'severe', first began to develop.

5. METHOD

Derived from the Latin *methodus*, meaning a 'way of doing' or 'teaching', the word *method* dates from the fifteenth century in English and was originally used to describe a prescribed or defined process or technique. In this sense, the word was first used purely in medical contexts to refer to the recommended course of treatment that should be taken in order to remedy certain conditions or diseases. Later use of the word became more generalized, referring simply to any technique of doing something, whilst in reference to 'regularity' or 'orderliness', the word dates from the early seventeenth century.

6. MORTIFYING

Adopted into English from French, the verb *mortify* originated in the fourteenth century and is ultimately derived from the Latin word for 'death', *mors*. In this sense, the verb originally meant to 'put to death' or 'destroy', and was first recorded as such in John Wycliffe's English translation of the Bible *c*.1382. As an adjective, however, the first use of the word *mortifying* was originally a medical one, used to describe either a caustic medical compound that could corrode flesh or tissue, or else a part of the body afflicted by a destructive, necrotizing condition like gangrene. In this sense, *mortifying* dates from the fifteenth century and it was not until the early seventeenth century that it came to mean 'humiliating' or 'deeply embarrassing'.

7. PLETHORA

Used to describe a vast amount of something, the word *plethora* is a Latin loanword ultimately descended from the Ancient Greek word for 'fullness', *plethore*. It first appeared in English in medical contexts in the mid-sixteenth century to describe an imbalance in the blood or any of the other bodily humours of historical medicine. This meaning broadened in the seventeenth century to come to refer to anything unhealthy or generally damaging to the body, and then, in the mid-nineteenth century, to an excess or overabundance of something. *Plethora* is in fact one of several English words whose meanings derive from the four traditional humours of ancient medicine: *revulsion*, for instance, originally referred to the withdrawal of such fluids from the body as a medical treatment, whilst *repulsive*, *repellent* and *repercussive* all once described anything used to drive bodily fluids back to their source and away from an injury or infection.

8. RECIPE

Unlike in modern English, the word *recipe* was originally a verb, first recorded in the early 1300s and derived from the Latin verb *recipere*, meaning 'to take', from where *receive*, *receipt* and *reception* are all similarly descended. As a verb, *recipe* was used exclusively in medical contexts as a direction written at the top of a prescription instructing a patient how best or how often to take their medicine. The noun *recipe* began to develop from this original meaning in the early 1500s, first simply as another word for a medicinal formula or compound, and then in the early 1600s in reference to a list of ingredients needed to prepare something.

9. REFRIGERATE

As modern as words like *refrigerate* and *refrigerator* may appear, they in fact have a considerably lengthy history with their earliest derivatives dating as far back as the fifteenth century. *Refrigerate* was originally an adjective rather than a verb, and meant simply 'chilled' or 'cooled', whilst both *refrigerator* and *refrigerative* were originally used to describe anything – and in particular a medicine – that had a cooling effect on a fevered person. The origin of all of these terms and others like them is the Latin verb *refrigerare*, meaning 'to reduce the temperature of' or 'to bring down an inflammation', which is itself derived from the Latin word for 'cold', *frigus*.

10. SPORADIC

The word *sporadic* has been used in English since the mid-nineteenth century to describe anything occurring intermittently or randomly, but prior to this it was used exclusively in medical contexts to refer to a non-epidemic outbreak of a disease, or else one of which only a handful of isolated cases are known. In this pathological sense, the word dates back as far as the late 1600s, and is derived at length from the Greek word *sporadikos*, meaning 'scattered' or 'sown', and ultimately the Greek for 'seed', *spora*, from which the English *spore* is also derived.

XXXVI

TEN WORDS DERIVED FROM PUNISHMENTS

Besides the ten words listed here that have all since slipped into more general use, the English language contains a number of much more unusual words for different methods of punishment and execution that are seldom encountered outside of historical contexts. For instance, as well as DECIMATION, in Ancient Rome *fustuarium* was the name of a military punishment reserved only for deserters of the Roman Army or for soldiers found guilty of dereliction of duty, who were flogged or cudgelled to death; in the Persian Empire, *scaphismus* was the name of a gruesome punishment in which the victim would be sealed between two log boats so that only his head and limbs were free, and then tormented with stinging and flesh-eating insects; and in the sixth century BC, the tyrannical Phalaris of Sicily was so famous for his cruelty – he introduced the 'brazen bull' as a method of execution, and even executed its inventor in it in order to test it out – that the term *Phalarism* came to be used in the sixteenth century to refer to any inhuman cruelty or torture.

I. DECIMATION
Derived from a Latin word, *decimatio*, literally meaning 'to remove one-tenth', historically *decimation* was a punishment meted out on mutinous or cowardly troops in the Roman Army in which men were rounded up into groups

of ten, with lots drawn amongst each group to select one man who was then promptly put to death by his nine cohorts. A comparable punishment, *vigesimation*, saw one in every twenty men killed, whilst in *centesimation* it was one in every hundred. Today, *decimation* is typically used in a much more general manner to mean simply 'destruction' or 'devastation', particularly of a large portion of something, but this less specific use of the word is often frowned upon by critics and more fussy speakers of English.

2. DEFENESTRATION

In modern English, the word *defenestration* is occasionally used in a figurative sense to refer to the removal of an individual or individuals from a high-ranking office. Strictly speaking, however, to *defenestrate* literally means to 'throw something or someone out of a window', and is ultimately derived from the Latin word for 'window', *fenestra*. This somewhat unusual term has its origins in the so-called Defenestration of Prague in 1618, in which two Catholic Lord Regents and one of their assistants were thrown from the third-floor window of Prague Castle by a group of Protestant noblemen, who were enraged at what they saw as the removal of various religious freedoms in Bohemia.

3. KEELHAUL

In maritime history, *keelhauling* was an extraordinarily brutal method of punishment administered on board ships in which the victim was tied to a rope that looped around the entire vessel, then thrown overboard and dragged either along or around the keel of the ship. Often the victim would drown or even be decapitated in the process, but if he did survive, the rough barnacle-covered base of the ship would nonetheless inflict terrible injuries. In this literal sense, *keelhaul* first appeared in the language in the mid-seventeenth century, but in modern English it tends only to be used in a metaphorical sense meaning 'reprimand severely'.

4. OSTRACISM

In Ancient Greece, the process of *ostracism* was a democratic procedure in which the people of Athens could vote to have one of the city's inhabitants banished for a period of ten years. The term derives from the Greek word *ostrakon*, meaning a 'tile' or 'piece of pottery', on which the name of the person in question would have been written; the unfortunate person whose name appeared the most would ultimately be expelled from the city. The modern use of the word, in the sense of shunning or excluding someone from a group, dates from the late 1600s.

5. PILLORY

Used to mean simply to 'deride' or to 'humiliate' since the seventeenth century in English, the *pillory* was originally an instrument of punishment and humiliation dating from medieval times, in which the victim was made to place his head and hands through holes in a wooden board, which was then locked shut, holding him in place, uncomfortably stooped over. Often erected in some communal location like a marketplace or crossroads, the *pillory* was usually placed on a raised platform to make the victim's punishment as public and as humiliating as possible, and leaving him open to the physical and verbal abuse of the people nearby. It was abolished as a form of punishment in Britain in 1837.

6. ROUÉ

As another word for a lecherous or debauched man, *roué* has been used since the late eighteenth century in

English. It is a derivative of the French verb *rouer* which, although essentially meaning 'to beat up' in modern French, historically meant 'to break on a wheel', referring to an ancient European method of capital punishment dating from the Middle Ages in which a victim would be strapped across the spokes of a huge wooden wheel and bludgeoned to death. Apparently such a punishment was once considered appropriate for someone exhibiting lecherous or lewd behaviour.

7. SEND-UP

Use of the word *send-up* to mean a satirical spoof or mockery of something is believed to have developed from English public-school slang, wherein *send-up* originally meant to be sent to the headmaster either for a reward or, more typically, for punishment. In this context, the word dates from the early nineteenth century – it appears in the works of authors including William Makepeace Thackeray and Thomas Hughes, in his *Tom Brown's School Days* – and remains in use at certain English public schools today.

8. SWEATBOX

Often applied metaphorically to any uncomfortably warm and enclosed environment – and in the 1970s to an unusual piece of weight-loss equipment – the earliest recorded use of the word *sweatbox* in English dates from the mid-nineteenth century. It described a narrow cell, used especially in arid desert regions, into which a prisoner was placed in solitary confinement as a punishment. The extreme heat and dry conditions outside the cell would cause temperatures inside to rise to dangerously high levels, making it extremely unpleasant and potentially fatal for the detainee. In this context, the term probably originated during the American Civil War.

9. SWELTER

The word *swelter* has been used since the fifteenth century in English to mean simply to 'suffer the heat', 'languish' or 'sweat'. It is derived from an earlier Old English word, *swelt*, which meant to 'die' or 'be overcome', but both words are ultimately related to an Old Norse word, *svelta*, which meant 'to be put or starved to death', which is still found in this sense in Icelandic today.

10. TREADMILL

Use of the word *treadmill* as a piece of exercise equipment dates from the 1950s, but the word itself was coined much earlier than that by the English inventor Sir William Cubitt, a Norfolk-born millwright and a former President of the Institute of Engineers. Cubitt's *treadmill* comprised a large cylinder, with a number of boards or steps around its edge, which could be made to turn by a person or group of people treading on the steps. Although the contraption had a wider industrial application in easing laborious tasks like raising water or grinding grain or rocks, the device was nevertheless put to use as a punishment in nineteenth-century prisons, wherein inmates were made to trudge away on the mill for hours at a time. Having been imprisoned for gross indecency in 1895, Oscar Wilde recounted being made to work the *treadmill* in *The Ballad of Reading Gaol*: 'We banged the tins, and bawled the hymns / And sweated on the mill, / But in the heart of every man / Terror was lying still.'

XXXVII

TEN WORDS DERIVED FROM WEAPONS AND WARFARE

The ten words listed here were all originally used in specific military contexts in English before gaining broader use elsewhere in the language. As well as being the origin of these and many more words like them, military English is also one of the most fruitful and inventive sources of English slang and colloquialisms. The First World War alone is the birthplace of terms like *civvy* (shortened from 'civilian'), *ammo* ('ammunition'), *recon* ('reconnaissance'), *conchy* ('conscientious objector'), *AWOL* ('absent without leave'), *monkey suit* ('uniform'), *washout* (a 'useless, ineffectual person'), and *Blighty* (a nickname for Great Britain), as well as the phrases to *get in a flap* (meaning to 'panic') and to be *on the mat* (to be 'in trouble with the authorities'). The Second World War, meanwhile, provided English with such terms as *snafu* ('mistake'), *shufti* ('glance'), *boot camp* (training area), *gremlin* ('bug or glitch in a system'), *prang* ('crash'), *brassed off* ('annoyed', 'fed up'), *sad sack* ('outsider', 'inept person'), *bogey* ('unidentified aircraft'), *God-bothering* ('overly religious'), *recce* ('reconnaissance'), *stateside* ('in America') and *trigger-happy* ('overly prepared to shoot').

1. BELFRY

It is a misconception that *belfries* are so named because they contain bells, as the word is in fact derived via

French from a considerably earlier Germanic word, *bergfrid*, which referred simply to a defensive shelter. The word *belfry* itself first appeared in English in the early fourteenth century with this original meaning still essentially intact, and originally described a movable wooden tower used by besieging forces in attacking castles and similar fortifications, which could be used to shelter the attackers. Later and in more developed forms, a *belfry* was an offensive siege engine in its own right. Over the years, the use of the word in English expanded to refer to any similarly tall shelter or watchtower, and eventually to a bell-tower, with the first part of the word changing through association from *ber-* to *bell-* sometime in the fifteenth century.

2. BLOCKBUSTER

Most often encountered today in reference to anything hugely successful or extravagant, the original *blockbuster* was in fact an enormous aerial bomb, so named as it was intended to be large enough to destroy an entire block of buildings. Developed by the Royal Air Force in the early 1940s, the first *blockbuster*, weighing 4,000 lb, was used during an attack on Emden in Germany in 1941. Although it was at the time the largest incendiary ever used by British forces, within just two years the RAF had begun using bombs three times this size, dropping more than 25,000 *blockbusters* weighing 12,000 lb in raids on Germany in 1943 alone. Popularized by the press, use of the word *blockbuster* soon caught on, with the first figurative reference to the entertainment industry dating from 1957.

3. BOMBARD

Although today it is almost exclusively used as a verb, meaning to 'barrage' or 'attack', the word *bombard* was in fact originally a noun in English, used in a variety of different senses and contexts to refer to a type of leather bottle or jug used to carry liquor; a wooden medieval musical instrument similar to a bassoon; and an early type of cannon used to fire rocks or large stones. It is from this latter meaning, first recorded in the language in the early 1400s, that the verb *bombard* eventually derived. Indeed, the verb itself was originally used to mean 'strike with a bombard', or 'assault' or 'destroy' with shot.

4. BRANDISH

Dating from the Old English period – and first recorded in the Anglo-Saxon poem *Beowulf* in the late tenth century – *brand* was an ancient word for a sword, or else the blade or main body of a sword or similar weapon. In turn, the verb *brandish*, which dates from the mid-1300s in English, originally meant to 'wave' or 'flourish a sword', presumably as a sign of aggression or intent to attack, or else in preparation for its use. Over time, its use became more general and eventually it came to mean simply to 'display' or 'flaunt'.

5. BREAKTHROUGH

Although the phrase *to break through* dates as far back as the fifteenth century in English, the compound noun *breakthrough* is a surprisingly modern addition to the language, first attested as recently as 1918. In this sense, the word was originally used only in military contexts to refer to the forward advancement of troops through a 'break' in an enemy's defensive line; the first recorded use of the word comes from a report of English and French troops making 'an attempted break-through' of the German front line in the final days of the First World War. Use of the word has since become much less specialized in English, with the first reference to a 'technological breakthrough' dating from the late 1950s.

6. INFRASTRUCTURE

Adopted into the language from French in the late nineteenth century, the word *infrastructure* was originally used only in military contexts in English to describe the various fixed buildings and installations, and all of their necessary foundations and subsystems, that are required for the running of a military operation, such as airfields and hangers, roads and bridges, training areas and mess halls. Use of the word soon became less specialized, however, and eventually came mean simply the basis or framework for any undertaking, and in particular the essential facilities and amenities required for the successful organization of a town or city.

7. MAGAZINE

Derived via French and Italian from the Arabic word for 'storehouse', *makzan*, the original meaning of the word *magazine* in English was, similarly, a 'repository' or 'place for storing goods', and in particular one used for the storage of ammunition, explosives, arms and other weaponry. Indeed, listed amongst the word's numerous alternative meanings and uses are several other military senses including a 'supply ship' (1620s), 'chamber of gun' (1670s) and 'container holding the bullets of a repeating firearm' (1868). As a metaphorical 'storehouse' of information, *magazine* first came to refer to a periodical publication in the eighteenth century, with the earliest recorded example being the *Gentlemen's Magazine*, first published in London in January 1731.

8. ORDERLY

Although the adverb *orderly*, meaning 'methodical' or 'well-organized', dates from the fifteenth century in English, the noun *orderly* dates back to the mid-1700s and was originally used to describe either a non-medical attendant in a military hospital or a military 'batman' or so-called *orderly corporal*, a personal assistant or attendant working in the service of a higher-ranking officer. The modern medical sense of an *orderly*, namely someone charged with maintaining the cleanliness and smooth running of a hospital, developed from the first of these two military meanings in the early nineteenth century.

9. PARK

Meaning a 'public common' or 'open area of land', the word *park* dates from the Middle English period and originally entered the language from an equivalent French term, *parc*, in the early 1200s. The verb *park*, however, dates from the mid-1500s in English and first meant to 'accommodate' or 'encamp troops' on a *park* or similar open expanse of land. It was not until the mid-nineteenth century – and originally in the United States – that the term came to refer to the positioning of a vehicle in an allotted place, a sense first used in reference to wagons (1840s) and then trains (1860s), before the first reference to a car being *parked* was recorded in a collection of short stories by P. G. Wodehouse, *Carry On, Jeeves*, published in 1925.

10. SMOKESCREEN

In its original sense the word *smokescreen* described precisely that – a screen of smoke intentionally produced by military forces either to conceal themselves or to disguise or divert the enemy's attention away from their operations. First recorded in reference to naval strategy 1915, the word soon gained a broader sense, denoting anything intended to distract or divert attention, in the 1920s. The verb *smokescreen* dates from 1950.

XXXVIII

TEN WORDS DERIVED FROM PEOPLE

Words derived from the names of real-life figures are actually quite numerous in English, ten examples of which are listed here. Sometimes, however, words claiming some kind of connection to a famous person are in fact unfounded. The *Caesarean section*, for instance, is popularly claimed to be named after Julius Caesar who was said to have been born by the method, but in fact the word is simply a derivative of the Latin word *caedere*, meaning 'to cut'. Nor is the nineteenth-century plumber Thomas Crapper (who also, despite popular opinion, did not invent the flushing toilet) the origin of the word *crap*, and nor is *shyster* the surname of a genuine unscrupulous lawyer but instead an alteration of a German vulgarism, *Scheisser*, for an awful or idiotic person.

I. CHAUVINISM
Although it is now almost exclusively associated with sexism, the word *chauvinism* originally described an intensely loyal and exaggerated patriotism, especially from a viewpoint that is blind to any opposition or alternative. The word is of French origin, and is derived from the name of Nicolas Chauvin, a (perhaps fictitious) French soldier whose blind patriotism to Napoleon's empire became legendary throughout France. First recorded in English in the late nineteenth century, by the mid-1900s use of the word *chauvinism* had generalized to imply any

194

extreme devotion or loyalty to a cause, particularly at the expense of other people's views – *male chauvinism* was first recorded in 1935, *female chauvinism* in 1970 and *cultural chauvinism* in 1975.

2. DUNCE

Dunce is derived from the name of John Duns Scotus, one of the most significant British philosophers and theologians of the Middle Ages. Born in Berwickshire *c.*1266, Scotus studied in Oxford and Paris before moving to Cologne in 1307, where he died the following year; his grave is famously inscribed with the words, 'Scotland brought me forth. England sustained me. France taught me. Cologne holds me.' His works on logic, philosophy and religion were held in high regard by medieval thinkers, but later scholars were less approving and eventually attacked and ridiculed his ideas. As a result, his followers, known as *Dunsmen* or *Dunses*, ultimately became associated with a lack of learning or an opposition to new thinking, and from the 1580s onwards *dunce* became just another word for a dim-witted person.

3. EPICURE

An *epicure* is someone with a refined and informed taste in food and drink. The term derives from Epicurus, a fourth-century BC Greek thinker whose school of philosophy, known as *Epicureanism*, rejected what he saw as a superstitious fear of the gods and their punishments, and instead focused on the enjoyment of a life unconcerned with fear of death and retribution. Although he explored much deeper philosophical ideas in many of his works – including the groundbreaking notion that the world was driven by the interaction of atoms – Epicurus's devotion to a carefree life led to the term *epicure* being used in the mid-sixteenth century for a glutton or hedonist, the sense by which it appears in Shakespeare's *Macbeth* (V. iii), before the less derogatory sense of the word still used today developed in the early seventeenth century.

4. GUILLEMET

Better known as 'angle quotes', *guillemets* are the symbols '«' and '»' used as speechmarks in a number of different languages including French, Italian, Greek and, in some countries, Arabic. In English, *guillemets* can be found in a handful of manuscripts dating up to the mid-sixteenth century when they were largely superseded by quotation marks. Today they are seldom encountered outside of their less familiar use in computer programming. *Guillemet* is a derivative of *Guillaume*, the French equivalent of 'William', and so it is presumed that *guillemets* took their name from that of an unidentified printer who devised them – the sixteenth-century French engraver Guillaume Le Bé is just one of several figures thought to have inspired the term.

5. PINCHBECK

As a slang name for a miserly, penny-pinching person, the word *pinchbeck* dates from the mid-1500s in English, but this use of the word (which is of uncertain origin) has long since fallen out of use. Dating from the mid-1700s, however, *pinchbeck* is also the name of a form of brass developed by and named after the London-based clock and watchmaker Christopher Pinchbeck, which contains a relatively higher proportion of copper to zinc than many other brasses, giving it a brighter, more golden colour. This made *pinchbeck* a popular replacement for gold in the eighteenth century, frequently used to make cheap jewellery as well as counterfeit coins and similar items, and ultimately in the late eighteenth and nine-teenth centuries the word came to be used to describe anything fake or of little value.

6. PRALINE

A true *praline* is a confection made by browning almonds or similar sweetly flavoured nuts in boiling sugar, although today the word is typically used to describe a sweet paste of chocolate and ground nuts often used as a filling for sweets or desserts. In its original form, *pralines* derive from César, comte du Plessis-Praslin, a seventeenth-century French diplomat whose personal chef at the Château de Vaux-le-Vicomte in Maincy, near Paris, invented the *praline*, or *prasline*, in the 1660s.

7. RADAPPERTIZATION

A radiation treatment used as a form of food preserva-tion, the odd word *radappartization* derives from the name of the eighteenth- to nineteenth-century French confec-tioner and scientist Nicolas François Appert who invented the process in the 1920s. Other processes and techniques derived from the names of their inventors include *mercer-ization*, a method of strengthening and brightening cot-ton developed by the nineteenth-century English chemist and printer John Mercer; *kyanization*, a chemical process for preserving wood from decay, patented by John Howard Kyan in 1832; *Grangerization*, the illustration of a book by its reader, often by pasting in pictures cut from other published works, popularized by the eighteenth-century writer James Granger; and, perhaps most famously of all, *pasteurization*, a method of food steriliza-tion pioneered by the French chemist Louis Pasteur in the mid-nineteenth century.

8. SAMARIUM

Chemical element number 62, *samarium* (Sm) is a silvery lanthanide metal, typically used in the manufacture of magnets like those found in headphones and in the pick-ups on electric guitars. It was discovered in 1879 by the French chemist Paul Émile Lecoq de Boisbaudran, yet derives its name from the radioactive mineral from which it was isolated, *samarskite*. This in turn is named after Vasili Samarsky-Bykhovets, a nineteenth-century Russian engineer and official who granted access to the mines in the Ural Mountains in which *samarskite* was eventually discovered in 1839. Although he was not physically involved in the discovery of either substance, Samarsky nevertheless remains the first person to have a chemical element – albeit indirectly – named after him. Other famous figures commemorated in the periodic table include Marie and Pierre Curie (*curium*, Cm, 96), Albert Einstein (*einsteinium*, Es, 99), Alfred Nobel (*nobelium*, No, 102), Ernest Rutherford (*rutherfordium*, Rf, 104), Nicolaus Copernicus (*copernicium*, Cn, 112) and the nineteenth-century Russian chemist, Dmitri Ivanovich Mendeleev, who is immortalized on the very table he helped formulate in the name of the element *mendelevium* (Md, 101).

9. SAXOPHONE

The saxophone, one of the largest instruments in the woodwind family, was invented by and named after the Belgian musician and instrument-maker Adolphe Sax, who patented its design in 1846. It is just one of a number of musical instruments to bear the name of its inventor, with other examples including the *sousaphone*, a large circularly coiled tuba named after the American bandleader John Philip Sousa; the *Wurlitzer*, a type of electric organ or similar keyboard instrument developed by Rudolph Wurlitzer in Cincinnati; and the *Moog*, a type of electric synthesizer invented by the American engineer Robert A. Moog in the 1960s.

10. TEDDY

Teddies – or, more fully, *teddy bears* – take their name from that of American President Theodore Roosevelt. According to the story, the *teddy* traces back to an event of 1902 when Roosevelt, then only in the second year of his presidency, was on a hunting trip to Mississippi. All members of the party except the President had apparently succeeded in killing something during the trip and so not to leave him out, a young black bear was caught, subdued and chained to a tree for sport. Roosevelt, however, refused to shoot the animal point blank and instead demanded that another member of the hunting team shoot it so as to 'put it out of its misery'. Despite showing Roosevelt in a compassionate light, satirists soon seized upon the event and famously a cartoon depicting Roosevelt 'drawing the line in Mississippi', his back turned to a bear on the end of a leash, was published in the *Washington Post*. Supposedly, the image inspired a New York toymaker named Morris Michtom to make a stuffed bear that he sold in his shop in Brooklyn as 'Teddy's bear'.

XXXIX

TEN FIRST NAMES IN THE DICTIONARY

The ten entries listed here are all familiar first names – from ABIGAIL and ANDREW to JIMMY and JOHN – that can be used in English as words in their own right. Whilst some of these terms are derived in some way from the names in question, often the similarity is coincidental and both the name and its alternative meanings are etymologically entirely unconnected.

I. ABIGAIL

Derived from the Hebrew for 'father rejoices', the first name *Abigail* has been used in English since the early 1600s as another word for a female attendant or maid. Use of the name in this context derives from the Bible, wherein *Abigail* was the humble wife and handmaid of King David, but in the early eighteenth century it was further reinforced by the appointment of Lady Abigail Masham as one of the chambermaids and eventual royal favourites of Queen Anne. This association eventually led several notable authors including Jonathan Swift, Charles Dickens and Henry Fielding to christen a number of maids and servants in their works *Abigail*, amongst them Miss Abbey Potterson, the schoolmarmish landlady of the Six Jolly Fellowship-Porters pub in Dickens's *Our Mutual Friend*.

2. ANDREW

Andrew is derived from the Greek word for 'man', *andros*, which is the same root for words like *androgeny*, *anthropology* and *philander*. The name's somewhat general meaning led to its use in the seventeenth and eighteenth centuries in English as simply another word for a valet or manservant, but over time a number of more specific meanings have developed: a *merry-andrew* is another word for a fool or a clownish assistant, popularly claimed to be derived from the name of Andrew Boorde, the court physician to Henry VIII, whilst *Andrew* is also used as another name for a ship in Shakespeare's *The Merchant of Venice* (V. i) in reference to the *St Andrew*, one of two grand Spanish galleons captured by Walter Raleigh at Cadiz in 1596.

3. GEORGE

The name *George* is derived from the Greek for 'farmer' or literally 'earth-worker', and as such is descended from the same root as words like *geography*, *geometry* and *geology*. *George* has a number of different uses in English, including as a form of address for a male stranger; an exclamation of surprise or amazement, as in *by George!*; another word for a loaf of bread, a term once popularly used amongst Oxford University students; and a slang term for a one-year prison service. By far the most prolific use of the name in English, however, is as a nickname for various coins and items of currency – in the United States, a *george* can be either a twenty-five cent piece or a dollar bill, both of which bear the image of George Washington, whilst in Britain the name has variously been used as another name for a 'noble', worth 6s 8d (late 1500s), a half crown (mid-1600s), a golden guinea (late 1700s) and a pound coin (late 1700s), most of which bore an image either of St George or of one of England's many King Georges.

4. HELENA

Helena is the Latin form of the Greek name *Helen*, which is in turn derived from the Greek word for a torch, *helene*. In the sixteenth century, the name was used as another word for the unusual maritime phenomenon, *corposant*, in which a gaseous, luminous haze created by the ionization of air molecules in the electrical field produced by a thunderstorm appears around the topmost masts of a ship. Also known as *St Elmo's fire* (a corruption of the name 'Erasmus', the patron saint of sailors), the phenomenon's alternative name *Helena* derives, like the name itself, from an Ancient Greek tradition wherein a single such ball of light was known as *Helena*, and a pair were known as *Castor* and *Pollux*, after Helena's twin brothers in Greek legend.

5. HENRY

Named after the eighteenth- to nineteenth-century American physicist Joseph Henry, the *henry* has been the official SI unit for electrical inductance since 1946. As well as this, the name *Henry* – derived from an old Germanic name meaning 'home ruler' – has a number of other uses in the language, including as a type of rifle, named after the noted nineteenth-century Scottish gunsmith Alexander Henry, and as an early twentieth-century American epithet for a car, named after Henry Ford, the American industrialist and founder of the Ford Motor Company. In cockney rhyming slang, meanwhile, a *henry* can variously refer to a 'word' (*Henry the Third*), a 'motorcycle' (*Henry Fonda*, rhyming with 'Honda'), and the

202

'devil' (*Henry Neville*, a nineteenth-century euphemism for 'Hell', as in *HE*nry Nevi*LL*e).

6. JIMMY

Both *James* and its pet form *Jimmy* can be used in English as another name for a crowbar, presumably due to their similarity to the tool's eighteenth-century name *jemmy* and to the influence of the rhyming slang phrase *jimmy rook*, meaning 'hook'. *James*, which is the English equivalent of the Latin name *Jacob*, is derived from the Hebrew word for 'heel' as, according to the Bible, Jacob was born clutching the heel of his twin brother Esau. The biblical tale of Jacob's Ladder, meanwhile, led to burglars who use ladders to break into houses being known as *jacobs* in the nineteenth century.

7. JOHN

Of all first names to have alternative meanings in English, *John* (derived from the Hebrew for 'God is gracious') is perhaps the most productive. Amongst its many meanings, *John* can denote a policeman, a butler or manservant, a priest, an Englishman, a lavatory, a signature, a type of plant, an unknown person, a cuckold or hen-pecked husband, and even the client of a prostitute. In the vast majority of these senses, it is simply the commonness of the name *John* that has led to its use, but nonetheless some of these meanings do have more curious origins. The use of the word for a policeman, for instance, is based on an English corruption of the French word *gendarme*, whilst its use for a signature is derived from *John Hancock*, a former Governor of Massachusetts whose elaborate signature dwarfs those of all the other signatories on the American Declaration of Independence.

8. MATILDA

Written by the Australian poet Banjo Paterson in the mid-1890s, the Australian folksong 'Waltzing Matilda' tells the story of an itinerant traveller or 'swagman' who sets up camp 'by a billabong / Under the shade of a coolabah tree', where he steals and kills a 'jumbuck' (sheep), before drowning himself in the waters when the 'squatter' (farmer) and three 'troopers' (policemen) confront him. It ends, 'And his ghost may be heard as you pass by that billabong: "Who'll come a-waltzing Matilda with me?"' The song is renowned for its use of many traditional Australian words and phrases, including those in its title: *waltzing* does not mean 'dancing' here but rather 'wandering' or 'journeying' (derived from the German expression *auf der Walz*, meaning 'to travel from job to job'), whilst despite popular belief *Matilda* is not the name of the swagman's sweetheart but rather his bag. Derived from an old Germanic name meaning 'mighty in battle', quite why *Matilda* has this meaning in Australian slang is unclear, but it has been suggested that travellers often gave their belongings female nicknames as they were essentially their only companions on their otherwise solitary journeys.

9. OLIVER

The name *Oliver* is thought to have entered into use in English either as a variant of the Scandinavian name *Olaf*, as a descendant of the Germanic name *Alfihar* (literally meaning 'elf-host'), or else as a derivative of the Latin word for an olive tree, *olivarius*. Whatever its origin, the word has since developed a number of different uses in the language, including as the name of a type of tilt hammer used in ironworking; an eighteenth-century slang name for the moon (presumably due to the shape of the letter O); a deliberate mistake entered into a book-keeper's ledger (from rhyming slang *Oliver Twist*, meaning 'fist'); and, as found in Chaucer's *Canterbury Tales*, an alternative name for the olive tree itself. *Oliver* and *Roland* together can also be used to refer to any equally or ideally matched pairing, as they were the names of two favourites of the Roman Emperor Charlemagne who, having been unable to beat each other in combat, were considered all but invincible together.

10. PAUL

Derived from the Latin *paullus*, meaning 'little' or 'small', the name *Paul* was recorded as far back as the mid-sixteenth century in English as the name of an Italian gold coin struck during the reign of Pope Paul III, which also bore an image of St Paul. More recently, *Paul* is also the name of a device used to trap ions named after its inventor, the twentieth-century German physicist Wolfgang Paul. Besides these somewhat obscure uses, *Paul* also appears in various words and expressions referring to St Paul's Cathedral – a *Paul's foot*, for instance, is an obsolete unit of measurement equal to the length of the foot of a statue of Ethelgar, a tenth-century Archbishop of Canterbury, found in St Paul's; a *Paul's-walker* is a gossipmonger or timewaster who would typically be found chattering in the nave of St Paul's; and *Paul's work* is a mess or a botched job, such as that that would be done by a *Paul's-walker*.

XL

TEN MAGIC WORDS

The ten entries listed here are all considered magic words either in the sense of a magician's performance or trick, like HOCUS-POCUS and ALAKAZAM, or else were believed at some time to have genuine magical properties, like ABRACADABRA and ABRAXAS. Many words like these date back many thousands of years, with mystical and protective powers often said to be instilled in words and phrases that exhibit some unusual characteristic. One of the most famous of all such phrases is the so-called Sator Square, a five-by-five square of letters containing the Latin palindrome *sator arepo tenet opera rotas* arranged in such a way so that the same phrase reads up and down the columns as well as along the rows. Although the phrase itself is all but untranslatable – *arepo* is found nowhere else in all existing Latin texts and its meaning is open to considerable debate – its unusual linguistic properties seem to have made it a popular slogan in Roman times. It has been discovered inscribed on stones located as far apart as Britain, the ancient Roman border city of Dura-Europos in Syria and the ruins of Pompeii.

I. ABRACADABRA

Long associated with magic and conjuring, in its earliest appearance in written language *abracadabra* was literally considered a 'magic word' believed to have special healing powers, as outlined in a third-century medical textbook, *De medicina praecepta*, by the Roman scholar Serenus Sammonicus. In the work, which comprises more than 1,500 lines of hexametric verse, Sammonicus lists a number of ancient cures and treatments, and explains that in order to cure a malarial fever a patient should be made to wear an amulet around their neck with ABRACADABRA written atop it, then ABRACADABR written below that, then ABRACADAB, ABRACADA, and so on with one letter clipped from the end of the word on each successive line until just A is left at the bottom, forming an upside-down triangle of letters. As Sammonicus eventually explains, 'Tie this about the neck with flaxen string, / Mighty the good 'twill to the patient bring.' Quite how *abracadabra* is invested with magic powers, and where the term itself comes from, is unclear – a connection to the Latin *abecadarius*, 'alphabetical order', has been suggested – but on its first appearance in English in the mid-1500s the word was similarly considered to have some manner of magical powers, which eventually led to its use in the early nineteenth century as a conjuror's exclamation.

2. ABRAXAS

The ancient word *abraxas* was historically used both as a magical spell in its own right and as the name of a talisman on to which the word *abraxas* would be written or carved for good luck. Borrowed into English from French in the early 1700s, the word and its apparent magical powers derive from the beliefs of a second-century Gnostic sect known as the Basilideans, who in turn adopted the word from Ancient Greek as the name of a deity they believed was in command of the 365 heavens. Whether the Greeks too thought the word had supernatural powers is plausible but uncertain, however it has been suggested that the word's seven letters were perhaps meant to represent the seven planets known since antiquity, whilst in isopsephy – the Ancient Greek practice of assigning numerical values to the alphabet – the letters of *abraxas* notably total 365: A (*alpha*, 1) + B (*beta*, 2) + R (*rho*, 100) + A (1) + X (*xi*, 60) + A (1) + S (*sigma*, 200) = 365.

3. ALAKAZAM

The word *alakazam* dates from the early 1900s in English and, as a magician's exclamation, is typically used to bring attention to the climax of a trick or, more generally, to any sudden change or action. Although popular folk etymology claims that the word is somehow derived from the Arabic *al qasam*, meaning 'the oath', in fact the true origin of *alakazam* is considered a mystery. It could even be an arbitrary creation coined simply to sound exotic or enigmatic.

4. HOCUS-POCUS

The word *hocus-pocus* dates back as far as the seventeenth century in English when it was variously used as a general name for a conjuror or juggler, as another name for a trick or sleight of hand and as the words of some fantastical magic spell or charm. This latter meaning appears to be the earliest of the three as the term was likely coined as some kind of faux Latin incantation by ancient conjurors and magicians, but the precise origins of the word remain unclear. If it is not merely some random formation, *hocus-pocus* could be derived from the name of *Ochus Bochus*, a forest-dwelling demon in Norse legend; the equally nonsensical faux-Latin phrase *hax pax max Deus adimax*, also used by magicians; or, perhaps most likely of all, a corruption of the Latin *Hoc est corpus meum*, 'this is my body', words used in the Catholic Eucharist.

5. KARAKIA

First described in English in the early nineteenth century, *karakia* are Maori prayer-like incantations, usually recited in a rapid monotone, that were used in practically all aspects of Maori life. Dozens of different types of *karakia* exist, from those used by Maori priests to communicate with the gods to those used in traditional Maori medicine and *makutu,* sorcery or witchcraft. Individual *karakia* included those used before battles, as greetings in ceremonies, as love charms, as aids to childbirth, to help ward off bad luck, to wish for fair weather, to help cleanse the homes of the deceased and even to help mend broken bones.

6. PASSE-PASSE

Derived from an old-fashioned French phrase once much used by jugglers and as a magic word by conjurors and tricksters, *passe-passe* is an obscure term first recorded in English in the seventeenth century as a synonym for sleight of hand or trickery, or for any skilful manipulation or movement. Also known as a *tour de passe-passe* (a French phrase for a conjuror's trick), the word is derived from a quirky reduplication of the French verb *passer,* meaning 'to pass'.

7. PRESTO

Often used as a musical direction, *presto* is an Italian word for 'quickly' or 'hurriedly' that has been used since the late sixteenth century in English as an expression or exclamation accompanying any sudden movement. In the early eighteenth century, magicians and conjurers picked up the term – often as part of the phrase *hey presto* or *hi presto* – as an expression emphasizing the climax of a trick, whilst in the nineteenth century *presto* became a verb in its own right, meaning to 'move' or 'transform' as if by magic.

8. SESAME

Quite why the treasure-filled cave in the story of *Ali Baba and the Forty Thieves* should be opened with the magic words *open sesame* is unknown, although it has been suggested that the words are meant to imply that the door would have split open like the shell of a crushed sesame seed. Whatever the meaning behind it, so familiar is the story of Ali Baba that the phrase *open sesame* has since entered into everyday use in English as an expression, often used humorously, to accompany something opened with a flourish. Since the nineteenth century, meanwhile, *sesame* has be used figuratively in English as another name for any password used to gain access (or attempt to gain access) to something prohibited or closed.

9. SHAZAM

Shazam was first attested in English in a Captain Marvel comic strip dating from February 1940. Although it is likely that the term was already being used by stage magicians and conjurors at the time, this first written record of *shazam* nonetheless offers a neat explanation of its origin: as described in *Whiz Comics #2*, the orphan Billy Batson encounters a dying wizard named Shazam, who offers the boy the opportunity to become his new champion. Billy accepts, and the wizard asks him to say his name, 'Shazam!' 'As Billy speaks the magic word,' the story continues, 'he becomes Captain Marvel', and is now is able to call upon the wisdom of *S*olomon, the strength of *H*ercules, the stamina of *A*tlas, the power of *Z*eus, the courage of *A*chilles and the speed of *M*ercury.

10. TETRAGRAMMATON

The word *tetragrammaton*, literally meaning a 'word of four letters' in Greek, has been used since the fifteenth century in English to refer to *YHWH*, the approximate English equivalent of the four Hebrew letters *yodh*, *he*, *waw* and *he*, which in ancient Hebrew biblical texts dating back as far as the ninth century BC was used as the proper name of the God of Israel. As biblical Hebrew was written using only consonants, however, precisely what the letters *YHWH* was intended to spell out is unknown and some traditions have since proposed that the actual name of God is unpronounceable. Nevertheless, in the Middle Ages, some sorcerers and magicians imagined that the true name of God, if it ever were to be known, would potentially be the most powerful magic word ever known and so used various approximations of the *tetragrammaton* in their spells. By the seventeenth century, the name *tetragrammaton* came to be used more generally to describe any magical symbol or charm consisting of four letters.

XLI

TEN ANIMAL NAMES

A number of animals' names are amongst the earliest recorded words in the entire English language. Predictably, a great many of them are the names of domesticated animals like *dog, cow, sheep, ewe* and *ram,* as well as animals that would have been caught or hunted for food, like *hare, goose, crab, hart, herring* and *eel,* although some other wild animals' names are of comparable age, including *rat, wasp, adder, fox, butterfly, seal* and *swan.* All of these examples date from the Old English period in the language, and are more than 1,000 years old.

Some of the earliest recorded names for animals, however, are also amongst the most unusual, yet many of them have long since dropped out of use. *Dive-dop,* for instance, was an Old English name for a grebe or diving duck; *attercop* was an old name for a spider, literally meaning 'poison cup'; *mire-drum* was a fourteenth-century name for the bittern, a bird of the heron family, thought to refer to its unusual booming call; and *angletwitch* was a wonderfully evocative Old English word for a worm used as bait on a hook. Ten more unusual and imaginative animals' names are listed here, many of which make similar reference to some supposed characteristic or ancient use for the creature in question (FATHER-LASHER, WART-BITER) whilst others refer to its shape or appearance (HELLBENDER, SNAKELOCKS).

I. FATHER-LASHER

A *father-lasher* is either one of two species of North Atlantic fish, *Taurulus bubalis* and *Myoxocephalus scorpius*, native to the seas around Britain, Ireland and much of the rest of northern Europe. First recorded in English in the seventeenth century, the name *father-lasher* refers to the fact that the male fish are known to lash out with their tails when threatened, especially whilst guarding their eggs during development. Also known as the *long-spined* and *short-spined sea scorpions*, despite these somewhat alarming names the creatures are in fact harmless to humans and grow little more than 10 to 15 cm (4 to 6 inches) in length.

2. GOATSUCKER

Goatsucker is an old English nickname for the nightjar, *Caprimulgus europaeus*, a peculiar nocturnal bird of Europe, Asia and Africa with incredible camouflaged plumage, a large gaping mouth and an unusual ticking or 'churring' song. The name pertains to the once widely held belief that the birds drank the milk (or even blood) of livestock at night, a misconception apparently based on nothing more than the birds' fondness for nesting in the same fields in which livestock are grazed as they like to feed on the flies and other insects that they attract. Dating from the early seventeenth century in English, the name *goatsucker* has its origins in Ancient Greece and Rome when the notion that the birds fed on cattle was first propagated by scholars including Aristotle and Pliny the Elder.

3. HELLBENDER

The *hellbender* is a species of giant salamander, *Cryptobranchus alleganiensis*, native to a large stretch of the eastern United States extending from New England down to Georgia, Alabama and Mississippi. Typically growing to more than 60 cm (2 ft) in length, with a round, flat head and a squat, bulky body, the *hellbender* is the third largest salamander in the world and one of the largest amphibians in all of North America. The origin of its name, which was first recorded in English in the early 1800s, is open to considerable debate but seems likely to be somehow intended to reflect the creature's ugly appearance.

4. HUNDRED-PACER

Hundred-pacer is a common name for *Deinagkistrodon acutus*, a stout, well-camouflaged 1 to 1.5 m (3 to 5 ft) nocturnal pit viper, also known as the *sharp-nosed viper*, which is native to parts of Vietnam, southern and eastern China, and Taiwan. The snake's unusual name refers to the fact that its venom is supposedly so potent that once bitten, a victim will only be able to take around a hundred paces away before dying; indeed, in some locations the creature is even referred to as the *fifty-pacer*.

5. PICK-A-TREE

Dating from as far back as the early 1600s, *pick-a-tree* is an old northern English dialect name for the woodpecker (and in particular the green woodpecker, *Picus viridis*), which alludes to the bird's habit of poking holes into the trunks of trees – the word *pick* here does not mean 'choose', but rather is an old English variant of *peck*. The green woodpecker is perhaps one of the most plentifully named of all British birds, with other alternative English names for it including *rainfowl* (mid-1400s) and *rainbird* (1550s); *woodwall* (late 1400s), *hickwall* (early 1500s) and *witwall* (mid-1600s); *woodspite* (mid-1500s); *yaffle*

(1700s), *yuckle* (1800s) and *yaffingale* (early 1600s); and *popinjay* (1800s).

6. SHOVELNOSE

The descriptive name *shovelnose* is shared by a number of predictably blunt-faced creatures of several different species, including a type of sturgeon found in the Mississippi and Missouri rivers, a burrowing frog of tropical sub-Saharan Africa, and a type of salamander native to North America's Appalachian Mountains. The earliest of all *shovelnoses* in English, however, is an otherwise unidentified species of shark first mentioned in 1707 in a work by the English seafarer William Funnell recounting his travels around the world as chief mate to the explorer and circumnavigator William Dampier. According to his account, Funnell spotted a 'shovel-nos'd-shark' as they were sailing south down the coast of Guatemala, and described it as having a head 'like a collier's shovel', with 'two extreme parts (at the edge of which on each side are his eyes) . . . a great deal broader . . . than his body'. Although the exact species of shark to which Funnell was referring remains unknown, based on his description it seems likely that it was one of the five species of hammerhead shark that are now known to inhabit the coastal waters of Central America.

7. SKELETONIZER

Skeletonizers are insects – or, more specifically, insect larvae – that feed so voraciously on leaves that they have earned their impressive name from their ability to reduce a leaf to just its skeleton in a short space of time. In English, the name was first recorded in an American dictionary of 1891 that referred specifically to the apple-leaf skeletonizer (*Choreutis pariana*), a moth native to much of North

America and Europe. A number of similarly named creatures exist, including the maple-trumpet skeletonizer (*Catastega aceriella*), the skullcap skeletonizer (*Prochoreutis inflatella*) and the Western grapeleaf skeletonizer (*Harrisina americana*), which can prove particularly destructive to grapevines in North American vineyards.

8. SNAKELOCKS

The *snakelocks* is a type of sea anemone, *Anemonia viridis*, native to the north-eastern Atlantic Ocean including the waters around the western side of the British Isles and the Mediterranean Sea. Its name makes reference to the anemone's long, snake-like tentacles, which are typically green or pale brown in colour with purple tips, and can reach more than 20 cm (8 inches) in length. Unlike many other anemone species the *snakelocks'* tentacles are almost always extended into the water.

9. SUNANGEL

The *sunangel* is any one of several species of tropical hummingbird native to a broad expanse of the western-most fringes of Amazon rainforest, stretching from Colombia in the north to Bolivia in the south. The common name *sunangel* is mirrored by the name of the genus to which all nine known species of the birds belong, *Heliangelus*, which is ultimately derived from the Greek word *helios*, meaning 'sun'. Other evocatively named hummingbirds include the *visorbearer*, the *sabrewing*, the *firecrown*, the *thorntail* and the *starfrontlet*.

10. WART-BITER

The *wart-biter* is a large species of bush-cricket native to much of continental Europe – including a handful of sites in the south of England – and across temperate regions of Asia to China. Growing to around 3 to 4 cm (1 to 1.5 inches) in length, the *wart-biter* resembles a grasshopper in appearance but tellingly, like all bush-crickets, produces its singing call by rubbing its wings together rather than by rubbing its legs against its wings as do grasshoppers. Its fairly gruesome name – which is reflected by the creature's taxonomic name, *Decticus verrucivorus*, derived from the same Latin root as *verruca* – originates in the Swedish name *vårtbitare*, as the cricket's powerful jaws were once widely used in Scandinavia to remove warts from the skin.

XLII

TEN THINGS YOU DIDN'T KNOW HAD NAMES

Estimates of the size of an average person's vocabulary range from a conservative 35,000 (which is still 4,000 more than William Shakespeare used) to 50,000 words, with knowledge of anything up to 75,000 words typical amongst people of higher education, and 100,000 or more characteristic of people like writers and editors, language scholars, crossword enthusiasts and professional Scrabble players. Given that the full twenty-volume *Oxford English Dictionary* contains around a quarter of a million individual words – excluding inflected forms like plurals and a great many more technical and regional words that have never fully established themselves in print – even the highest of these estimates fall far short of the entire extent of the English language. Unsurprisingly then, dictionaries contain a great many words whose meanings are not widely known, of which ten that perhaps deserve to be more widely known are listed here.

1. ACNESTIS
Derived at length from *knestis*, the Ancient Greek word for the spine or backbone (and also, oddly, a cheese-grater), the *acnestis* is the part of the back that cannot be easily reached to scratch, typically said to be the region located between the shoulder blades. The *acnestis* is just one of a number of body parts whose proper names are

rarely used or not widely known – the *glabella*, for instance, is the flat bare region of the forehead between the eyebrows; the *philtrum* is the small groove in the top lip just below the nose; the *canthus* is the corner of the eye, the point at which the eyelids come together; and the *lunule* is the proper name for the white, crescent-shaped mark found at the base of a fingernail or toenail.

2. AGLET

An *aglet*, or *aiglet*, is the name of the metal tag or coated tip found at the end of a shoelace, intended to make the lace easier to thread through the eyeholes of the shoe. First recorded as early as the fifteenth century, the word was borrowed into English from French, and was originally a diminutive form of the French word for 'needle', *aguille*.

3. BORBORYGM

First recorded in English in the early 1700s, a *borborygm* or *borborygmus* is a rumbling sound produced in the stomach or intestines, typically caused by excess air or liquid as it is moved through the gut by *peristalsis*, the natural muscular contractions that push food through the digestive tract. The word is derived from the Ancient Greek name for this phenomenon, *borborygmós*, which is believed to be an example of onomatopoeia, invented in imitation of the rumbling noise itself.

4. INTERFENESTRATION

Coined in the nineteenth century in line with the earlier seventeenth-century architectural term *intercolumnation* (describing the space between the pillars of a building), an *interfenestration* is the space formed between two windows; something described as *interfenestral*, ultimately, would be located in such a space. Derived from the Latin preposition *inter*, meaning 'between' or 'amongst', of similar origin are the equally obscure English words *inter-arboration*, referring to the interweaving of the branches of two trees; *interdigitation*, the 'interlocking of the fingers of clasped hangs'; and both *interanmian* and *inter-lacustrine*, a pair of adjectives describing either land enclosed by or situated between two rivers or two lakes respectively.

5. LALOCHEZIA

Formed from the Greek word for 'speech', *lalia*, and the unusual Greek verb, *khezo*, meaning 'to defecate', *lalochezia* is proper name for the use of vulgar language as a means of emotional relief, and so can be used to describe the profanities with which a person instinctively comes out when, for instance, they are in pain or shocked. The word is related to the more widely accepted psychological term *coprolalia*, coined in the late nineteenth century by French physician Georges Gilles de la Tourette, which refers to the spontaneous and involuntary use of obscene language as associated with sufferers of Tourette's syndrome.

6. NUDIUSTERIAN

Dating from the mid-seventeenth century in English, something described as *nudiusterian* occurred the day before yesterday; the word is based on the Latin phrase *nunc dies tertius est*, literally meaning 'now is the third day'. The obsolete English term *ereyesterday* means precisely the same thing, whilst the adjective *hestern* or *hesternal* describes something that happened yesterday. Oppositely, the old word *crastin* is an alternative name for tomorrow; the *overmorrow* is the day after tomorrow; and the verb *perendinate* means to 'put off until the day after tomorrow'. Despite their potential usefulness, all of these terms are very rarely used in English.

7. PEEN

The *peen* is the dull, rounded end of a hammer, the end opposite the larger and heavier 'head' or 'face' used to strike nails. First recorded in the seventeenth century (but dating from the early sixteenth century as a verb meaning 'strike with a hammer'), *peen* is believed to be of dialect origin in English, and perhaps originally derived from some long lost French or Scandinavian word.

8. PETRICHOR

Coined in an article published in the scientific journal *Nature* in 1964, the word *petrichor* is formed from the Greek word for 'rock' or 'stone', *petra*, and *ichor*, the name used for liquid said to flow through the veins of the gods in Greek mythology. The word describes the pleasant, earthy odour that can be smelt in the air following the first rainfall after a prolonged period of dryness, which is formed by an oil naturally produced by leaves during dry weather. Over time, this oil is absorbed into the soil and rocks under the leaves and is released by the rainwater into the air, creating the distinctive *petrichor* smell.

9. PHOSPHENE

Derived via French from the Greek words *phos*, meaning 'light', and *phainein*, meaning 'to appear' or 'to be revealed', *phosphenes* are the 'lights' caused by artificial or mechanical stimulation of the retina when no actual light is present – that is to say, *phosphenes* are the 'lights' you see when you rub your eyes or close them tightly. The phenomenon is generally understood to be triggered by a slight increase in pressure within the eyeball when it is rubbed or closed, which automatically stimulates the receptive cells of the retina, thereby giving the illusion of light. *Phosphenes* can also be caused by stimulating the retina electronically, using electrodes to pass a current into the visual cortex of the brain, which can even create 'lights' in the eyes of some blind people.

10. QUAALTAGH

A *quaaltagh* is the first person you meet after leaving your home. Dating from the nineteenth century, the word is one of only a handful to have been adopted into English from the Manx language of the Isle of Man, where local folklore maintains that the identity of the *quaaltagh* is of great importance to what is to come. This is especially true at or around Christmas and New Year, and indeed the term is also used as an alternative name for a 'first-footer', the first person to enter a house on New Year's Day.

XLIII

TEN PORTMANTEAUX

Also known simply as 'blends', portmanteaux are words formed by combining two or more pre-existing words, usually (but not always) the first part of one and the second part of another. The process has remained a popular and inventive means of creating new words for centuries, with some early examples even including major place names like *Czechoslovakia* (Czech + Slovakia), *Tanzania* (Tanganyika + Zanzibar) and *Budapest,* formed from the unification of the earlier cities of Buda and Pest in 1873. Some more modern portmanteaux, however, can appear fairly clumsy – *hoolivan* is an odd 1980s name for a police van used to observe football crowds, and *affluenza* was a 1970s psychiatric term referring to a depressive condition affecting prosperous young people – and are often frowned on by more conservative speakers.

The word *portmanteau* itself dates from the sixteenth century as the name of a type of suitcase or holdall, and was originally borrowed into English from French, where it was used to refer to an attendant or servant who would carry (*porte*) a person's cloak (*manteau*). It was the author Lewis Carroll who first used the term in reference to blended words in his 1871 work *Through the Looking-Glass,* stating, 'You see it's like a portmanteau – there are two meanings packed up into one word.'

1. BALLOONATIC

A blend of *balloon* and *lunatic*, the word *balloonatic* dates from the mid-nineteenth century in English, when it was first used simply to describe someone who is obsessed with hot-air ballooning and other dirigibles. During the First World War, it gained an alternative meaning in military slang when it was used as a nickname for members of the Balloon Squadron who were in charge of airships, barrage balloons and observation balloons. A considerably earlier term, *balloonomania*, dates back as far as the late eighteenth century and was coined in the years following the Montgolfiers' first public displays of their hot-air balloons in France in the 1780s.

2. BUTTERCUP

Buttercup, the common name for the plant *Ranunculus* and its familiar bright yellow flowers, was first recorded in English in the late 1700s. Despite a popular folk etymology claiming that the flower's name refers to the notion that butter acquires its bright yellow colour from cows feeding on *buttercups*, in fact the plants are poisonous to livestock. The name is instead simply a blend of two considerably older names for the plant, *gold-cups* and *butter-flower*, both of which date back to the sixteenth century.

3. CAJOLE

Meaning to 'coerce' or 'persuade', especially through flattery or obsequiousness, the verb *cajole* has been used in English since the mid-seventeenth century. First adopted into the language from French, the word's earlier history and etymology are uncertain. With no apparent single source, it has been suggested that *cajole* was perhaps originally a blend of two earlier French verbs, *enjoliver*, meaning 'to make pretty', and *cageoller*, meaning 'to chatter like a jay or a bird in a cage'.

4. CYBORG

The word *cyborg* is formed from a blend of the phrase 'cybernetic organism', its coinage typically credited to the American scientist (and acclaimed classical pianist) Manfred Clynes. First recorded in 1960, Clynes, in collaboration with fellow scientist Nathan S. Kline, initially used the term to refer to an organism combining both biological and artificial parts, and in particular talked of a mechanically enhanced human being that could withstand long periods in space and so could be used to work in extra-terrestrial environments. *Cyborgs* were, Clynes theorized, necessary for humanity to reach further into outer space.

5. FANTABULOUS

A blend of 'fantastic' and 'fabulous', *fantabulous* is one of a vast number of creatively and humorously coined adjectives and adverbs now used in English, most dating from the mid- to late twentieth century. Other examples of this type include *humongous* (perhaps based on 'huge' and 'monstrous') and *ginormous* ('giant' and 'enormous'), *absotively* and *posilutely* (both formed from 'absolutely' and 'positively'), *scuzzy* ('scummy' and 'fuzzy'), *snazzy* (perhaps 'snappy' and 'jazzy') and *bodacious* ('bold' and 'audacious').

6. NETIZEN

First recorded as far back as 1984 but popularized in the 1990s and early twenty-first century, the word *netizen* is formed from a blend of the phrase 'internet citizen', and as such is used somewhat light-heartedly to refer to someone who participates in online communities and discussions, or else simply someone who uses the internet; the equivalent term *cybercitizen* dates from 1994. *Netizen* is one of a number of humorous and colloquial coinages dating from the eighties and nineties that pertain to computer use, including *netiquette*, referring to appropriate online conduct; *netocracy*, a perceived online democracy (or aristocracy); *screenager*, a teenager adept at using computers and other technology; *vidiot*, the computer or online equivalent of a couch potato; and *hacktivist*, a protestor who hacks into an organization's computer files.

7. RUCKUS

The word *ruckus* has been used to refer to a commotion or violent confrontation since the late nineteenth century, although during the Prohibition era in the United States in the early 1900s the word also came to be used as a slang term for strong but poor-quality alcohol, typically known as *rookus* or *ruckus juice*. Apparently an American coinage, the word is presumed to be a blend of *ruction* and *rumpus*.

8. SITCOM

The entertainment industries are the source of a vast number of blended words, of which the 1960s American coinage *sitcom* – a 'situation comedy' – is just one. Indeed, in reference to film and television alone, the English language now contains such as terms as *mockumentary* (US, 1980s), *rockumentary* (US, 1960s) and *shockumentary* (US, 1970s); *edutainment* (US, 1980s), *docutainment* (US, 1970s) and *infotainment* (US, 1980s); *docudrama* (US, 1960s) and *docusoap* (UK, 1970s); *infomercial* (US, 1980s) and *advertorial* (US, 1910s); and both *prequel* (US, 1950s)

226

and *threequel* (US, 1980s), first used in reference to *Jaws 3-D* in 1983.

9. SMOG

Formed from a blend of 'smoke' and 'fog', the word *smog* was first recorded in English in 1905 and is believed to have originally specifically applied to the polluted atmosphere of London. Of similar meaning are both *smaze*, a blend of 'smoke' and 'haze' first coined in 1953 to describe the smoky air of Manhattan, and *vog*, a portmanteau of 'volcanic smog' first recorded in 1987 to describe the choking fumes almost continuously released by Hawaii's Kilauea volcano.

10. ZEDONK

A *zedonk* is the offspring of a male zebra and a female donkey. First recorded in 1971 when such a creature was born at Colchester Zoo in Essex, the word is one of a number of similar terms for other so-called zebroid creatures, including the *zonkey*, the *zebrass*, the *zorse* and the *donkra*, the offspring of a donkey and a female zebra, a rare example of which was born at Haicang Zoo in China in 2011. In fact, the English language contains an assortment of portmanteaux names for similarly hybridized animals, the most familiar examples of which are probably the *liger* and *tigon*, the offspring of a lion and a tiger, and domestic breeds like the *labradoodle* (a Labrador and poodle cross) and the *goldendoodle* (a golden retriever and poodle cross). Amongst many less familiar examples, however, are the *jagupard* (the offspring of a male jaguar and a female leopard), the *wholphin* (the offspring of a whale and a dolphin), the *coywolf* (from a coyote and wolf) and the *beefalo*, the offspring of a domestic cow and an American bison.

XLIV

TEN WORDS THAT WERE
ORIGINALLY PHRASES

The ten entries listed in this chapter are all formed from
the elision of the words of a full phrase rather than individual words. This type of formation is not as common
in English as straightforward portmanteaux, but is a
particularly fruitful source of so-called 'minced oaths',
euphemistic expressions and interjections that have
formed over time from the combination of the words of
a more controversial (and often religious) phrase. The
nineteenth-century expressions *blimey*, *gorblimey* and *gaw-
blimey*, for example, are all formed from the phrase 'God
blind me!'; *gadzooks* is a sixteenth-century term supposedly referring to 'God's hooks', the nails used to
fasten Jesus to the cross; *gadswoons* and *zounds* make
reference to 'God's wounds'; and both *criminy* and *jiminy*
are popularly said to be a euphemistic alteration of
'Christ's money' or 'Jesus's money', the thirty pieces of
silver accepted by Judas to betray Jesus to the Romans.

I. ALARM
On its first appearance in the language in the fourteenth
century, the word *alarm* was originally an exclamation
used as a call to arms. Descended via French from the
Italian phrase *all'arme*, meaning literally 'to the arms',
over time the use and meaning of the word developed to
come to refer to an actual call to arms itself – as in

Shakespeare's *Henry VI, Part 2* (V. iii), 'Whilst the angry trumpets sound the alarmes' – and, eventually to any sound or noise intended to rouse someone or stir them into action. The first recorded reference to an *alarm clock* comes from a lost-and-found notice printed in the *London Gazette* in 1697, reading 'Lost ... a Larum Clock in a little Box'.

2. AMPERSAND

Until as recently as the early 1900s, it was once common practice when reciting the alphabet in English to use the Latin phrase *per se* (literally meaning 'by itself') to differentiate individual letters of the alphabet from single-character words like *a* and *I*. Ultimately, the letter A would be *A per se*, the letter I would be *I per se*, and the letter O would be *O per se*, distinguishing it from the interjection *O!* As just another individual character, the symbol *&* was also once considered a letter of the alphabet and was included after Z, in twenty-seventh place, and recited as *and per se and*, thereby differentiating the symbol 'and' from the word 'and'. Sometime in the early nineteenth century, *and per se and* eventually combined into the single term *ampersand*, which has remained the name of the *&* symbol ever since.

3. CULPRIT

The word *culprit* has its origins in the old French legal phrase *Culpable: prist d'averrer nostre bille*, roughly translating as 'Guilty: ready to be proven of our charge'. Historically, this phrase was used in English courts as the stock response given by the clerk of the Crown when the accused entered a plea of not guilty. As the phrase was heard so frequently, in the court records it would be noted down just as *cul. prist*, and eventually this abbreviated form established itself as simply another word for the defendant, even after the use of French in English courtrooms died out in the seventeenth century. The word was first recorded in English in the court records of the trial of Philip Herbert, the Eighth Earl of Pembroke, who was accused of the murder of a man in a tavern brawl in 1678. Found not guilty of murder but guilty of manslaughter, Pembroke escaped prosecution through Privilege of the Peerage, and was simply ordered to pay all of the court fees incurred.

4. COUNTERVAIL

Effectively meaning 'counteract' or 'compensate for', the verb *countervail* is derived from the French *contrevaille*, which is itself descended from a contraction of the Latin phrase *contra valere*, meaning 'to be of worth against'; in fact, on its first appearance in English in the late fourteenth century, the word meant to be 'of equal value to'. *Countervail* is one of a number of English words that are descended from contractions of Latin phrases, including *antebellum*, literally meaning 'before the war'; *videlicit*, usually abbreviated to *viz.*, from the Latin *videre licet*, meaning 'it is permissible to see'; and *catacomb*, which is believed to be taken from the Latin *cata tumbas*, meaning 'amongst the tombs'. One explanation of the origin of the word *snob*, meanwhile, is that it is taken from a contraction of the Latin *sine nobilitate*, literally meaning 'without nobility', although this theory is now largely discredited.

5. EUREKA

Used since the sixteenth century in English as an explanation of discovery or triumph, *eureka* literally means 'I have found it' and is derived from Ancient Greek verb *heurisko*, meaning 'to find'; in fact, *eureka* should rightly be spelled with an initial H. Archimedes's famous use of the word – supposedly exclaiming it as he sat in a bathtub and saw the water level rise – alludes to a story in which he had been asked by the King of Syracuse to determine whether his crown was pure gold. As Archimedes discovered that the amount of water displaced by a submerged object is equal to its mass, he could work out the precise mass of the crown without damaging it, calculate what its density should be if it were indeed pure gold, and therefore assess whether or not it had been blended with any other metal.

6. FIAT
Dating from the sixteenth century in English, in basic terms a *fiat* is an authoritative command or an official decree demanding an action. The word itself is specifically the third-person singular present subjunctive form of the Latin verb *fio* meaning 'to become' or 'to make happen', which effectively makes it the Latin equivalent of the phrase 'let it be done'. Its use in English is likely reinforced by the familiarity of the biblical phrase *fiat lux*, meaning 'Let there be light'.

7. GOODBYE
First recorded in the language in the sixteenth century, *goodbye* is a contraction of the phrase 'God be with you'. The change from *God* to *good*, influenced by other expressions like *good day* and *good night*, was complete by the early late 1600s, with the first use of the abbreviated colloquial form *bye-bye* first recorded in 1709.

8. MONDEGREEN
A *mondegreen* is the misunderstanding of a phrase or lyric, caused by mishearing and misinterpreting the words that

it contains for others that sound identical. Appropriately, the word *mondegreen* itself is an example of precisely that – coined by the American writer Sylvia Wright in a 1954 article in *Harper's Magazine*, the word derives from Wright's childhood misinterpretation of the final lines of the popular Scots ballad 'The Bonny Earl O'Moray'. She mistook 'They have slain the Earl o' Moray / And layd him on the green', for 'They have slain the Earl o' Moray / And Lady Mondegreen'. Wright goes on to explain that, 'The point about what I shall hereafter call mondegreens ... is that they are better than the original'.

9. OHNOSECOND

Derived simply from the phrase *oh no*, an *ohnosecond* is the moment of time between making a terrible, irreversible mistake and realizing it. Coined in the 1990s, *ohnosecond* was first used in reference to computing, wherein the slightest of actions – such as deleting the wrong file or sending an email to the wrong person – can often have grave and irretrievable consequences, typically only realized the second after the damage has been done.

10. ULTRACREPIDARIAN

The extraordinary adjective *ultracrepidarian* essentially means 'extending beyond one's own knowledge', and is often used to describe critics and other commentators who offer misguided opinions on subjects of which they have no real knowledge or expertise. First recorded in the works of the English writer and critic William Hazlitt in the early 1800s, the word derives from the Latin *ne ultra crepidam*, literally meaning 'not beyond the sandal', a phrase taken almost word for word from an anecdote recorded in the works of the Roman scholar Pliny the

Elder. According to the story, a shoemaker once dared to point out that the renowned Greek artist Apelles had apparently made an error in painting a sandal on a figure in one of his artworks, an oversight which Apelles promptly corrected. Spurred on by this, the shoemaker went on to point out another apparent error in Apelles work, to which the artist is said to have replied, '*ne supra crepidam sutor iudicaret*', meaning 'a shoemaker should not judge above the sandal'.

XLV

TEN IMITATIVE WORDS

It is widely known that words invented to imitate the sound that they describe are known as onomatopoeia, a Greek term literally meaning 'the making of names'. As can be seen by the ten examples listed here, however, onomatopoeic words are not just limited to such simple words as *boom, pop, pow* and *whizz*, but can instead be used as the names of animals (BOOBOOK), as the name of musical terms (RATAMACUE, FANFARE) and as words in their own right (BOMBINATE, ULULATE). It has even been suggested that some innocuous words like *rake, owl, roar, laugh, rook* and even *pebble* – perhaps echoing the sound of a stone being dropped in water – could all have originally been intended to be imitative when they were first used in the Old English period.

1. BOMBINATE
Dating from the nineteenth century, the verb *bombinate* means 'make a buzzing sound'. It is derived from the equivalent Latin verb *bombitare*, which is itself a derivative of the Latin word for a humming or buzzing sound, *bombus*. This earliest Latin form is presumably intended to resemble the low droning sound to which it refers, and is thought to be the source of a whole host of similar English words including *boom, bomb* and *bombard*.

2. BOOBOOK

The *boobook* or *buckbuck* is a medium-sized owl native to central Australia, whose name is supposedly meant to be imitative of its somewhat unusual call. The bird is one of a vast number whose (often highly unusual) English names are said to emulate their calls, with other examples including the *wompoo*, an Australasian fruit dove; the *chiff-chaff*, a small migratory warbler found throughout Britain in summer; the *huia*, a now extinct bird of New Zealand with a long down-turned bill; the *kiewiet*, a South African lapwing; the *chowchilla*, a small thrush-like bird found in the tropical forests of Queensland; the *querquedule*, another name for the teal or pin-tail duck; the *dickcissel*, a North American meadow lark; and, perhaps most famously of all, the *cuckoo*.

3. BREKEKEKEX

The extraordinary word *brekekekex* was first recorded in English in the early 1600s. It was borrowed directly from *The Frogs*, a play by the Ancient Greek playwright Aristophanes first performed in 405 BC, in which the Greek god Dionysus travels into Hades to bring the play-wright Euripides back from the dead. Whilst crossing a lake in the Underworld, Dionysus engages in a lengthy debate with a chorus of frogs, who repeatedly call out *brekekekex, ko-ax, ko-ax!* Ultimately the word has been adopted into English as imitative of the croaking of frogs.

4. CLISHMACLAVER

Derived from Scots English and first recorded in the early 1700s, the word *clishmaclaver* means 'idle, empty talk' or 'prattle', or else can be used as a verb meaning simply to 'chat' or 'gossip'. It is believed to be formed from two earlier Scots verbs, *clish-clash* and *claver*, both of which also mean to 'talk' or 'chatter', with all three terms supposedly intended to imitate the sound of a casual, gossipy conversation.

5. FANFARE

A short, rousing or flourishing tune, typically played by bugles or horns, the word *fanfare* was first recorded in English as *famphar* in the early 1600s. Adopted into the language from French, the word is presumed to be of imitative origin, with the earlier equivalent French verb *fanfarer* perhaps intended to sound like the playing of a *fanfare* itself. At its very earliest, the word could be descended from the earlier Spanish word *fanfarrón*, meaning 'braggart' or 'swaggerer' (from which the obscure English words *fanfaron* and *fanfaronade*, meaning 'boastful, precocious blather', are both derived), which is itself perhaps intended to emulate to sound of bragging, blustering chatter.

6. OOMPAH

Imitating the repetitive, marching musical beat typically performed on a deep brass instrument, the word *oompah* dates from the late nineteenth century in English. More recently, it has come to be applied to the brash, bouncy style of music that characteristically uses this kind of jaunty bass rhythm, whilst *oompah* has even been used as a verb (meaning to 'perform an *oompah*') since the 1910s. The derived term *oom-pah-pah* dates from the 1930s and is intended to imitate a three-beat rhythm pattern, like that of a waltz.

7. PACHINKO

Pachinko is the name of a Japanese mechanical game similar to pinball, in which a small ball or series of balls is dropped through a vertical field of pins or pegs and into any one of a number of holes or slots below, with players aiming to capture as many of the balls as possible. Played primarily as a gambling game similar to a Western slot machine, *pachinko* is a hugely popular pastime in Japan with so-called 'pachinko parlours' often housing hundreds of individual devices. Its name, which dates from the 1920s or 1930s in Japan but has not been recorded any earlier than the 1950s in English, is said to be imitative of the sound of metal balls being struck and ricocheting away.

8. PLANXTY

Originating in Irish English, the unusual word *planxty* refers to a lively piece of music – or else a dance performed to such a tune – typically with a triplet beat and a quick tempo, and often played on a fiddle or a harp. Dating from the early 1700s, the precise origin of the word is unclear but it has been suggested that it is simply intended to imitate of the sound of the plucked strings of a harp. If this is not the case, however, *planxty* could instead be descended from the Latin verb *plangere*, meaning 'to strike' or 'to beat', or else it is perhaps a corruption of the Irish phrase *phlean an tí*, meaning 'from the house of', implying that such tunes were originally written and performed in domestic surroundings.

9. RATAMACUE

In music, the *ratamacue* is one of the most basic patterns or so-called 'rudiments' of drumming. Its name is supposedly imitative of the sound that the pattern itself produces, namely a triplet rhythm (the *ra-ta-ma*) followed by an accented fourth beat (the *cue*). Indeed, the *ratamacue* is just one of a number of similar standard rhythmic patterns used in drumming that have been given equally descriptive names, with others including the *flam* (a single drumbeat, in fact formed from two distinct beats played in quick succession); the *flamacue* (a set of four beats wherein the first and last are *flams*, and the second beat is accented); the *pataflafla* (a pattern of four repeated beats, the first and last of which are *flams*); and the *paradiddle* (four even beats, all but the second of which are played with the same hand). With the exception of *flam*, which dates from as far back as the eighteenth century, the majority of these terms are relatively recent additions to the language, with *ratamacue* itself dating from the early 1900s.

10. ULULATE

The verb *ululate* means simply 'howl' or 'wail', and dates in English from the early seventeenth century (although a related adjective, *ululative*, is recorded as far back as the 1400s). It is derived from an earlier Latin word of identical meaning, *ululare*, which was likely coined in imitation of the sound of a plaintive or lamenting cry and is thought to be related to the Latin name for the tawny owl, *ulula*, which is known for its screeching call.

XLVI

TEN WORDS WITH UNUSUAL ALTERNATIVE MEANINGS

It is obviously not uncommon for words to have more than one established meaning in the language, as often nouns and verbs can be used interchangeably (as in '*dance* a *dance*' or '*dream* a *dream*') and frequently the meanings of words develop and evolve over time to such an extent that they end up encompassing entirely new senses and contexts. In some cases, however, words can end up adopting very unusual meanings that, although still connected to their original or most familiar definition, can be somewhat surprising.

1. ANGEL

The first recorded use of the word *angel* in English comes from a tenth-century edition of the Lindisfarne Gospels, the word being formed from a blend of the existing Old English word *engel* and the Norman French *angele*, both of which are ultimately derived from the Latin word *angelus*. Since this initial appearance in the language, *angel* has developed several other related meanings in English, including 'spiritual guardian' (dating from the fourteenth century), 'messenger' (mid-fifteenth century) and 'beautiful or bright young person' (late sixteenth century). However, the word has also gained a number of much less familiar uses, including the name of an old English gold coin first minted during the reign of Edward

IV in the 1460s and, more recently, an American slang word for a financial backer. In the mid-1900s, however, *angel* slipped into use in British Air Force slang when it began to be used by RAF pilots to refer to a height of 1,000 ft, and later to any unexplained or transitory mark that appears on a radar screen.

2. ENVELOPE

Adopted from the equivalent French term *enveloppe*, the word *envelope* has been used in English since the early 1700s, and was first recorded in reference to the paper sheath into which a letter is placed in 1715. Besides this familiar use of the word, however, *envelope* also has a number of more obscure applications, most of which still bear some similar sense of an enclosure or containment: it can variously be the part of an airship or hot-air balloon that contains the air or gas; a set of limitations within which a machine or device can be operated safely; the *coma* or covering of the head of a comet; or the outer casing of a biological or anatomical structure, such as the head of a flower or the outer membrane of a virus. Perhaps the most unusual alternative use of the word, however, appears in reference to defensive architecture, wherein an *envelope* is a raised earthwork mound or rampart, typically built inside or in front of a ditch surrounding a fort, which is intended to protect a weak point in its defences and prevent it from being breached.

3. HAND

Predictably for such a familiar word, *hand* has a great many alternative meanings besides its most obvious one, amongst the least familiar of which is perhaps its use in reference to the authority a Roman husband had over his wife. In this sense, *hand* was first used in English in the late 1800s and is a direct translation of the Latin word *manus*, which was used in the same sense.

4. MATADOR

The word *matador*, the Spanish for 'killer', is all but entirely associated with bullfighting in English, and in this context was first recorded in the late 1600s. Of similar age, however, is the use of a *matador* in certain card games – and in particular trick-taking games like ombre, quadrille and skat – to designate the highest of the trump cards, often (but not always) including the ace of spades and the ace of clubs. More recently, in the nineteenth century, *matador* began to be used as a variation of the game of dominoes, in which players are permitted only to link tiles so as to form a total of seven; in this version of the game, tiles whose spots already total seven, like the 2-5 or 3-4, are all known as *matadors* and can be played at any point during the game.

5. MULE

As the name of a cross between a donkey and a mare, the word *mule* dates back to the Old English period and is ultimately derived from the equivalent Latin term, *mulus*. Characteristically strong and hard-working, these stereotypical features of the mule's temperament have led to its name being applied in various other senses in the language, including as the name of a small, powerful tractor or similar vehicle used to tow heavy loads (early 1900s); an American slang term for strong alcoholic liquor (1920s); and the name of a type of high sail, able to provide considerable pull to a yacht or similar vessel (1930s). The word is also used in several senses referencing the creature's hybrid nature, and can variously refer to a type of spinning wheel able to produce both thick and thin yarn (early 1700s); a coin with incorrectly mismatched obverse and reverse sides (early 1800s); and as a general term for a crossbred bird (mid-1800s) or sheep (late 1800s).

6. PACE

Referring either to the rate of walking or movement, or to the distance covered in a single footstep, the word *pace* dates back to the fourteenth century in English and is derived from the Latin word for 'step' or 'stride', *passus*. Although also used in a number of other contexts implying some sense of walking or moving – in the architecture of a church, for instance, a *pace* is a passage between rows of pews or chairs, whilst historically the word was used to refer to a route through difficult terrain – by far the most unusual use of the word is as the collective name for a group of asses or donkeys. As such *pace* is one of a number of everyday words used on rare occasions as a so-called collective noun. Besides familiar examples like a *pride* of lions or a *troop* of baboons, English speakers can also refer to a *shrewdness* of apes, a *siege* of heron, a *labour* of moles, a *descent* of woodpeckers, a *parliament* of owls, a *knot* of toads and a *bask* of crocodiles, besides many more.

7. RABBIT

The word *rabbit* was adopted into English from French in the fourteenth century and eventually all but replaced the earlier English term *cony* or *coney*, which today remains largely only in use in English dialects. Amongst the word's many alternative meanings, in the early twentieth century the word began to be used in Australian English as a nautical slang term for anything that has been smuggled or stolen, and ultimately *rabbit* can also be used as a verb meaning 'steal' or 'borrow'.

8. RUN

In 2011, *run* overtook *set* as the word with the most recorded definitions and senses in the *Oxford English Dictionary* – a record-breaking 645. Able to be used as a verb (dating from the early Old English period), a noun (from early fifteenth century) and an adjective (late fifteenth century), perhaps unsurprisingly for such a prolific word *run* has a great number of unfamiliar uses in the language. It can variously be used to refer to the rearmost part of a ship's hull; a pair of twin millstones; a rapidly played series of musical notes; a 1,600-yard length of yarn; a set of wagons in a coalmine; a discordant sound created by air leaking from one organ pipe into another; a number of livestock or other animals born at the same time; and the quantity of oil obtained during one period of extraction.

9. SKI

The first mention of a *ski* in English – borrowed into the language from Norwegian and descended from the Old Norse word for a snowshoe, *skið* – dates from the mid-1700s, with the verb *ski* and the practice of *skiing* first recorded in the late 1800s. During the Second World War, however, *ski* began to be applied to so-called 'ski sites', locations across Nazi Germany from where V-1 flying bombs and other long-range weaponry could be launched, which featured long, narrow, curved buildings and storehouses that from the air appeared to resemble skis. More than seventy of these sites were located by Allied reconnaissance during the course of the war, with many being destroyed by strategic bombing raids launched as part of Operation Crossbow in 1943–5.

10. VAMPIRE

As the name of a supernatural, blood-sucking monster, the word *vampire* has been used in English since the early eighteenth century, although stories of such creatures date back many hundreds of years more in the folklore of Eastern Europe; *vampire bats*, meanwhile, were first described in English in the 1770s. More recently, the word has gained a less familiar alternative meaning in the language of the theatre, wherein a *vampire* – or, more specifically, a *vampire trap* – is the name of a type of spring-loaded stage trapdoor with two covering doors, which allows a performer to make a sudden appearance or disappearance on to or off of the stage. This use of the word was first recorded in the 1880s, and is believed to have developed from the use of just such a device in an early nineteenth-century stage adaptation of the classic horror story *The Vampyre* by John Polidori.

XLVII

TEN FAKE WORDS

For decades, dictionary editors and compilers have often included entirely fictitious entries as traps intended to catch anyone seeking to copy and reprint the text as their own – if a faked entry were ever to appear in another dictionary, the original editors would know immediately that their work had been plagiarized. Such terms are variously known as *ghost words*, *nihilartikels* (literally 'nothing-articles') or *Mountweazels*, named after the fictitious Lilian Virginia Mountweazel whose entirely fabricated life story was included in the 1975 edition of the *New Columbia Encyclopedia*. Although some of the earliest of these ghost words were rooted in genuine lexicographical mistakes (like DORD and PHANTOMNATION), more recently they are the deliberate creations of editors and are included just as jokes or for publicity purposes. Nevertheless, despite their inaccuracy, some of these entries end up taking on a life of their own after publication and can remain in print for several years.

I. APOPUDOBALIA

The fictitious word *apopudobalia* was included in the first volume of the 1980 edition of the *Realencyclopädie*, a renowned German encyclopaedia of classical antiquity. In the book, *apopudobalia* was defined as an Ancient Greek sport similar to and considered a precursor of modern football, which was hugely popular amongst Roman legions and consequently spread throughout Europe as the empire expanded until it reached Britain, where 'the game enjoyed a revival in the nineteenth century'. The entire article, which even includes fake references to both ancient and modern scholarly texts, was a hoax.

2. DORD

The word *dord* was defined as meaning 'density' when it was included in the second edition of *Webster's New International Dictionary* in 1934. In fact, no such term has ever existed but it was not until five years after the book went to print that the mistake was noticed. According to the story, the entry was mistakenly created in July 1931 when a consultant specializing in chemistry terms sent a note to the editors of the dictionary reading 'D or d, cont./density'. The note was intended to mean that the word 'density' should be included in a list of words for which the letter D (or lower case d) can be an abbreviation, but instead 'D or d' was misread as a single word and entered into the text. A part of speech and even a recommended pronunciation were both subsequently added to the entry and the word went to print. It was not removed until 1947.

3. ESQUIVALIENCE

When the second edition of the *New Oxford American Dictionary* was published in May 2005, it was announced that alongside the addition of 3,000 new words this latest edition also featured a fake entry somewhere under the letter E. As reported in the *New Yorker,* the American journalist Henry Alford eventually narrowed this potential bogus entry down to a shortlist of six possibilities, and after consulting with several language experts eventually discovered the fictitious word *esquivalience.* Defined as 'the wilful avoidance of one's official responsibilities' or 'the shirking of duties', the word was said to have been coined in the nineteenth century from the (genuine) French verb *esquiver*, meaning 'to dodge', but in fact it had simply been concocted by one of the dictionary's editors.

4. FOUPE

Foupe was erroneously included in Samuel Johnson's landmark *Dictionary of the English Language* in 1755, in which it was defined as a verb meaning to 'drive with a sudden impetuosity'. Citing a quotation from an early seventeenth-century work by the English historian William Camden, both Johnson's definition and citation were correct, but his spelling of the word was not – he had misread the so-called long S (ſ) often used in texts dating from the time as a lower-case F (*f*), and so Camden's original quotation should have read, 'To soupe their words out of the throat with fat and full spirits.' The error was not corrected until the early nineteenth century, but *foupe* is still listed in the *Oxford English Dictionary* as 'an error for soupe'.

5. HIYBBPRQAG

In one of the most inventive uses of fake words, in 2011 Google used the fake search term *hiybbprqag* in an online sting operation against Microsoft and its rival search engine, Bing. As widely reported in the press at the time, Google had earlier become suspicious that Bing had been copying their search results after noticing similarities between the topmost results on both sites, despite inconsistencies in users' spelling. In one example, users who searched for 'torsoraphy' via Google had their spelling corrected to *tarsorrhaphy* (a surgical procedure carried out on the eyelids) before being directed to a list of relevant websites, whilst searching for the same misspelling via Bing did not correct the error, but still managed to produce the same results. In an attempt to uncover what was happening, Google created a list of around one hundred fake words, and linked each one to a different website – searching for *hiybbprqag* brought up a seating chart for a Los Angeles theatre. When it was discovered that searching for the same fictitious word brought up the same result in Bing, Google were able to prove that Microsoft had indeed been copying their results.

6. JUNGFTAK

A 1943 edition of *Webster's New Twentieth Century Dictionary* featured the word *jungftak*, defined as a 'Persian bird, the male of which had only one wing, on the right side, and the female only one wing, on the left side', so that the pair had to join together in order to fly. Unsurprisingly, both the creature and its name were entirely fictitious, but it was not until the 1980s that the hoax was uncovered and finally acknowledged by the dictionary's editorial staff.

7. PHANTOMNATION

Phantomnation was defined as meaning a 'multitude of spectres' in the *Philology of the English Language*, an 1820 work by the English classicist Richard Paul Jodrell. Jodrell took the word from an eighteenth-century translation of Homer's *Odyssey* by Alexander Pope, but in doing so removed a hyphen from Pope's original quotation describing 'the Phantome-nations of the dead'. As such, Jodrell accidentally created his own ghost word, which despite its inaccuracy went on to be adopted into a handful of other dictionaries, including Webster's 1864

American Dictionary of the English Language, which defined it as an 'appearance as of a phantom'. The *Oxford English Dictionary*, however, correctly refers to it as 'a misinterpretation' of Pope's term.

8. STEINLAUS

The *steinlaus*, or 'stone louse', was a fictitious creature invented by the German humorist and filmmaker Loriot for a 1976 comedy sketch parodying nature documentaries. In the film, Loriot describes the *steinlaus* as a recently discovered yet endangered species of mite, 20 to 24 mm in length, that is able to consume up to 28 kg (62 lb) of stone a day – the film even features footage of building demolitions that are attributed to the creature's insatiable appetite for rock. Seven years later, the joke was picked up by the editors of *Psychrembel*, a renowned German medical dictionary, who included the *steinlaus* as a fake entry in their 1983 edition. Loriot's original description was expanded to an even more ludicrous extent, with the editors assigning the *steinlaus* a scientific name (*Petrophaga lorioti*, 'Loriot's stone-eater'), describing its use in the treatment of kidney and bladder stones, and even suggesting that its unusual diet was partly responsible for the destruction of the Berlin Wall.

9. YITS

In 1953, the Yorkshire sport historian M. C. Norris included the word *yits* in his *Glossary of Northern English Dialect*, variously defining it as a noun, 'another name for a gardener's edging tool'; as a verb, meaning to 'hurl' or 'throw a great distance'; and as 'an exclamation of accomplishment, probably a variant of "yes"', which is 'essentially equivalent to *hurrah*'. Although the word does exist in standard English – both as a variant of *oats* and as a verb meaning to 'feed with oats' – Norris's use of it in his *Glossary* is fake. It was supported by a number of equally fictitious quotations supposedly taken from the works of various northern writers including Wordsworth, the Brontë sisters and the seventeenth-century Yorkshire poet Andrew Marvell.

10. ZZXJOANW

The word *zzxjoanw* – supposedly pronounced '*shaw*' – was included in a 250-page 'pronouncing and defining dictionary of terms, instruments etc.' featured in *The Musical Guide*, a 1903 reference work by the American historian and composer Rupert Hughes. Listed as a Maori word variously defined as a 'drum', 'fife' and 'conclusion', the word puzzled linguists and musicologists alike for decades, during which time it was reprinted in all editions of Hughes's book and was widely discussed and quoted in several other similar titles. After considerable debate, given the word's unlikely pronunciation, its random assortment of meanings and, crucially, the fact that the Maori language contains only fourteen letters (none of which are Z, X or J), *zzxjoanw* was eventually declared a hoax.

XLVIII

TEN FOLK ETYMOLOGIES

When the true etymology of a word is not known (and even sometimes when it is), it is common for a popular but entirely fictitious explanation of its origin to develop. Often, these so-called folk etymologies provide neater, cleverer, more intriguing or more humorous explanations than any genuine etymology could possibly provide, and so are popularly repeated and gain considerable currency despite their inaccuracies. Ten examples of stories like these, attempting to explain the origins of ten familiar English words, are listed here.

I. CABAL

In the late seventeenth century, the term *cabal* – or, more fully, the *Cabal Ministry* – was used to refer to a select group of the most central members of Parliament serving under Charles II, which are generally considered the precursors of what is today the Cabinet. Given this initial use of the word, it is often claimed that *cabal* is an acronym of the names of Sir Thomas Clifford, Lord Arlington, the Duke of Buckingham, Lord Ashley and Lord Lauderdale, the five chief ministers of Charles II's Parliament who signed the Treaty of Dover in June 1670, allying England and France in a potential war against the Netherlands. However, the fact that these five men's names and titles could be manipulated so as to spell *cabal* is entirely coincidental, and the word in fact dates back to the beginning of the seventeenth century as simply a shortened form of *Cabbala*, the name of the Jewish interpretation of the Old Testament.

2. GOLF

Besides the fact that it can be dated back to 1457 and is known to be of Scottish origin, the precise derivation of the word *golf* is one of the most persistent etymological mysteries in the whole of the English language. Perhaps the most likely explanation is that it is derived from a Dutch word for a club or stick used in ball games, *kolf*, yet even this is not without question – no Dutch games that used an implement called a *kolf* are thought to have been known by the same name, whilst the first use of *golf* in English predates the use of *kolf* in Dutch by a number of years making it unlikely that the one developed from the other. What can be said for certain, however, is that the popular explanation that *golf* is an acronym of 'Gentlemen Only, Ladies Forbidden' is assuredly untrue.

3. KANGAROO

The first recorded use of the word *kangaroo* in English dates from 1770 and the journals of Captain James Cook written whilst he was aboard HMS *Endeavour* on its first voyage to the South Pacific. A popular story explaining the word's origin claims that it is a native Australian term literally meaning 'I don't know', or, more realistically, 'I don't understand you' – supposedly when Cook saw *kangaroos* for the first time he asked a native what they were, to which they replied 'kangaroo'. As popular as this tale is, however, it has since been proven to be apocryphal as the word can be reliably traced back to the ancient Guugu Yimithirr aboriginal language of Australia, in which *gangurru* is the native name for grey kangaroos.

4. MARMALADE

One myth surrounding the origin of the word *marmalade* is that it was once served to Mary, Queen of Scots, after she had fallen ill during a visit to France. Supposedly, the queen overheard her maids say, '*Madame est malade*', literally meaning 'madame is ill', and mistakenly took this to be the name of the dish of stewed fruit that she had been served. Regrettably, this story is entirely untrue as *marmalade* in fact derives from the Portuguese word *marmelo*, meaning 'quince', the fruit from which the first marmalades would have been made. Moreover, the earliest record of the word in English dates back to 1480, more than sixty years before Queen Mary was even born.

5. NASTY

The origin of the word *nasty* is a mystery in English, although one commonly held explanation claims that it is derived from the name of Thomas Nast, a nineteenth-century, German-born American caricaturist and satirical artist, who is perhaps best today known for creating the famous elephant symbol used by the Republican Party. Known as the 'Father of the American Cartoon', in the mid-1800s Nast became widely recognized across the United States for the harshly critical and derisive nature of his work, much of which was printed in the renowned *Harper's Weekly* and *New York Illustrated News*, and so it is often claimed that anything said to be *nasty* is as similarly scathing or cruel as Nast's drawings. As neat as this story is, however, it cannot possibly be true as the word *nasty* in fact dates back to the fourteenth century.

6. POMMY

A humorous nickname for a British person used in Australia, New Zealand and South Africa, the word *Pommy* or *Pom* was first recorded in English in 1913. The origin of the word is unclear, although a number of different stories and tales attempting to explain its history have nevertheless developed over the years. Amongst them, it is often claimed that *Pom* is in fact as an acronym of the phrase 'Prisoner of Mother England', or else 'Prisoner of Her Majesty's Exile', as Australia was the destination for many convicts sentenced to transportation to the colonies in the nineteenth century. Another theory claims that the word is derived from the name of Pommery champagne, which was supposedly the drink of choice of English cricketers touring Australia in the early 1900s. Perhaps the most likely explanation, however, is that *Pommy* is simply a clipped form of *pomegranate*, used either as rhyming slang for 'immigrant' or in reference to the red, sunburned skin of Britons visiting Australia.

7. PUMPERNICKEL

One tale explaining the origin of *pumpernickel* bread claims that the word is derived from the French phrase '*bon pour Nicol*', or '*pain pour Nicol*', often attributed to Napoleon, which literally implies that the bread is only good enough for 'Nicol', a French nickname for a poor-quality horse. In fact, the word actually derives from German rather than French, although its true derivation is just as unusual: the first part of the name, *pumper*, is an old German equivalent of the English word 'fart', whilst the second, *Nickel*, is a derivative of the name Nikolaus, probably meant as a euphemistic name for the Devil, or 'Old Nick'. Quite why the bread should be named after the 'Devil's fart' is unclear, but it may simply be intended to imply that early *pumpernickels* were particularly difficult to digest.

8. SINCERE

Meaning 'honest' or 'heartfelt', the word *sincere* dates back to the mid-sixteenth century in English, and is correctly derived from the Latin adjective *sincerus*, meaning 'genuine' or 'pure'. Despite this somewhat straightforward derivation, popular folk etymology maintains that the word is, in fact, derived from the Latin phrase *sine cera*, literally meaning 'without wax', and indeed a number of fanciful tales supposedly supporting this idea have been concocted over the years: it is often claimed that sculptors in Ancient Greece and Rome were known to cover up cracks or other mistakes or imprecisions in their work with wax; that the Ancient Greeks would make gifts of wax statues and other implements which would be gifted to their enemies after a losing battle, but which would quickly melt in the heat of the sun; that wine bottles and documents without wax seals could not be trusted; and that wax was often used to fill out hollows in busts and similar objects sold to their buyers as solid gold or bronze. None of these tales, however, is true.

9. SIRLOIN

The cut of meat known as the *sirloin* takes its name from the French word *sur*, meaning 'above' (from which the word *surname* is also derived), and so the *sirloin* is simply the cut found 'above the loin' of an animal. Despite this simple explanation, folk etymology has it that the *sirloin* is so named as it was once knighted by King Charles II (although other monarchs are sometimes credited) for being such a superior cut of meat. This story is, however, untrue and in fact the word itself predates Charles's reign by more than a century.

10. SWORD

Found as *sweord* in Old English and recorded in a number of texts dating back as far as the tenth century, one persistent folk etymology of the word *sword* claims that it is a contraction of the expression 'God's word'. This explanation is often supported by the quote 'For the word of God is quick, and powerful, and sharper than any two-edged sword', lifted from the biblical Book of Hebrews (4: 12), but in fact *sword* is simply derived from its ancient Germanic equivalent, *swerdom*.

XLIX

TEN WORDS OF UNKNOWN ORIGIN

Despite the best efforts of linguists, researchers and lexicographers, a collection of words exists whose origins cannot be – and probably never will be – unequivocally explained. Ten such words, many of which began as colloquialisms or slang terms, are listed here along with their potential or most probable etymologies.

1. BLOKE

Perhaps surprisingly for such a familiar word, the origin of *bloke* remains a complete mystery; amongst several possible derivations and linguistic connections are the Romany or Hindi word *loke* (meaning 'man'), the Celtic word *ploc* ('large or stubborn person') and an old Dutch word *bloc* (meaning 'fool'). What is known is that the word can be traced back as far as the nineteenth century in English, and is believed by some sources to have developed as a slang term amongst London criminals in the early 1800s, when it seems to have first implied an owner, a master or a judge, with the more general sense of simply a 'man' developing shortly afterwards.

2. BOGUS

First appearing in English in the early nineteenth century, the word *bogus* was originally a noun rather than an adjective, and was used to refer to the machinery or apparatus used to make counterfeit currency. In this sense, the word has its origins in American slang, but its precise derivation before then is unclear. Of a number of attempted explanations, perhaps the most likely is that it is a shortened form of the earlier word *tantrabogus*, used in eighteenth- to nineteenth-century New England as a term for any odd-looking object, which is in turn probably derived from *tantrabobs*, an old West Country name for the Devil.

3. COCKTAIL

The earliest recorded use of the word *cocktail* in English dates back to the mid-1500s, when it was used to refer to a horse with a 'cocked-tail', that is to say, an intentionally shortened or docked tail that was often left as a stump sticking upwards like that of a cockerel. In reference to a mixed alcoholic drink, however, the word did not appear until the early 1800s, and in this sense the origin of the word is a mystery. It could be that the two meanings here are related, the implication being that the alcoholic content of a *cocktail* gives the drink a 'kick' at the end, much like that of the horse's upturned tail. Alternatively, the two forms could be entirely separate, in which case *cocktail* could be a derivative of the French word for an eggcup, *coquetier*, implying that such drinks would once have been measured out or served in small, individual cups. Either way, the history of the word remains a complete mystery.

4. CODSWALLOP

Meaning 'nonsense' or 'garbage', the word *codswallop* can be dated no further back than the mid-1900s in English, and is first attested in a 1959 edition of the BBC comedy series *Hancock's Half Hour*. Like a number of other humorous English terms – including *shenaningans*, *flabbergast* and *balderdash* – the origin of *codswallop* is a mystery, although a variety of different suggestions have been proposed. Amongst the most elaborate of these is the notion that *codswallop* is derived from the name of the nineteenth-century English engineer Hiram Codd, who in 1872 patented a type of bottle that uniquely used a marble to form a perfect seal against a rubber washer in the neck, which quickly became a widely used container for bottled mineral water and other soft drinks in the late Victorian era. *Wallop*, meanwhile, is recorded in the 1930s as a slang term for alcohol, and so the implication is that *codswallop* was originally a drinker's name for bottled water, or else any poor-quality beer or liquor. As convenient as this explanation first appears, however, the eight decades between the invention of Codd's bottle and the first recorded use of *codswallop* casts doubt on its likelihood.

5. GIMMICK

Today used to refer to a trick or contrivance, typically one intended to grab attention or garner publicity, the word *gimmick* dates from the 1920s in English when it was originally used as another name for a gadget or similar small device, and in particular one used to cheat in gambling or with which a magician performs his trick. The word first developed in American slang, but its precise etymology remains unknown – one potential derivation claims that it was originally formed as an anagram of 'magic', *gimac*, whilst another suggests that it is just an alteration of the much earlier term *gimcrack*, meaning a 'showy but trifling object'.

6. JAMBOREE

Amongst the Scout Movement, it is popularly held that the founder of the movement, Sir Robert Baden-Powell, invented the word *jamboree* for the first International Rally of Boy Scouts held in London in 1920. Baden-Powell, it is claimed, either created the word at random or else based it on some existing obscure word – such as the Swahili word for 'hello', *jambo*, or the Aboriginal Australian word for a meeting or loud celebrating, *corroboree* – of which he presumably had some knowledge. This explanation, however, cannot be correct as the word *jamboree* predates the formation of even the first of Baden-Powell's scout groups in 1907 by almost forty years, with its first recorded use in reference to rowdy celebration taken from an article in the *New York Herald* dating from 1868.

7. OK

The origin of *OK* is one of the most famous mysteries in whole of the English language, with dozens of different explanations of its history having been suggested over the years. Amidst the most fanciful (and the least likely) of these explanations is that *OK* derives from the French phrase *aux quais* (meaning 'to the docks'), which was once written on crates of exported cotton; Aux Cayes, a Haitian port from where good-quality rum was once imported; *Oberkommando* ('High Command'), a phrase used on communications endorsed the German head of the American Continental Army in the 1700s; *okeh*, a Native American Choctaw word meaning 'it is'; and even *och aye*, the familiar Scottish expression. Of all potential explanations here, however, the most likely appears to be that *OK* grew from a popular fad, traced back to the street slang of cities like Boston and New York in the 1830s, for abbreviating humorous misspellings of commonly used phrases: *OK* was probably an abbreviation of 'orl korrect', whilst *NC* was used to mean 'nuff ced', and *KG* meant 'know go'. As short-lived as this fad appears to have been, *OK* apparently survived its demise and in 1840 it was used as an electoral slogan by the US President Martin van Buren, whose nickname 'Old Kinterhook' (the name of his hometown) was abbreviated by his Democrat supporters to 'OK'. Although this history is generally taken as the most likely today, realistically even this can only be considered a best guess.

8. SNOOKER

The first recorded reference to the game of *snooker* in English dates from an 1889 book called *The Art of Practical Billiards for Amateurs*, in which it is described as a game 'which is not yet generally known, or much played'. The word *snooker* itself, however, predates this association with the game and was recorded in the 1870s as a jocular name for a newly enlisted army recruit. Where this word is originally derived from, and quite why the game should be so called are both unknown, although one suggestion popularly claims that whilst serving in India in 1875, it was Colonel Sir Neville Chamberlain (not the British Prime Minister, but rather a former British Army officer and Inspector-General of the Royal Irish Constabulary) who first applied the name to this variety of billiards, presumably jokingly highlighting another player's amateurishness or lack of experience of the game.

9. YONKS

Meaning 'a very long time', the word *yonks* was first recorded in English in the 1960s. Popular in British English but almost unheard of in North American varieties, the word is of unknown origin but is perhaps formed from an alteration of the colloquial phrase 'donkey's years' (which is in turn based on the rhyming slang *donkey's ears*). Alternatively, it could be an approximate combination of the word 'years', 'months' and 'weeks'.

10. ZIGZAG
Besides presumably being related to the earlier equivalent German word *zickzack* (used to refer to a zigzagging ditch or trench around a fort intended to be harder for the enemy to see into), little of any assurance is known of the origin of the word *zigzag*, which dates back to the eighteenth century in English. It has been tentatively suggested that the word *zigzag* itself is merely intended to be a representation of its meaning, the shape of the letter Z and the change of vowel in each neighbouring syllable said to imply the alternating lines of a *zigzag*, but no assured explanation of its origin has yet been determined.

L

TEN WORDS OF UNUSUAL ORIGIN

Finally, listed here are ten random words that, although they do not quite fit the brief of any of the preceding chapters, arguably have such interesting etymological stories to tell that they deserve to be included regardless.

1. CURFEW

Dating from the early fourteenth century in English, the word *curfew* was adopted into the language from the old Norman French term *coeverfu* or *couvre-feu*, literally meaning 'cover-fire', as historically *curfews* were regulations put in place in medieval Western Europe that demanded all domestic fires and candles be extinguished at a certain time in order to prevent fires from breaking out overnight. As these original *curfews* were typically signalled by the ringing of a bell late in the evening, long after the rule of extinguishing fires had dropped out of use the word *curfew* remained in the language simply as another name for any late-night signal or bell, or else as a directive restricting activities or movements after dark.

2. DEADLINE

The word *deadline* first entered the language as a nineteenth-century American military term describing a line drawn on the ground, either around or within the boundaries of a military prison, which if crossed, a prisoner would risk being shot. In this sense, the term was first used during the American Civil War, and became more widely known following the trial and eventual execution of a Swiss-born major of the Confederate Army named Henry Mirz. He infamously employed a *deadline* during his brutal command of Camp Sumter, a prisoner of war camp in Anderson, Georgia; more than a quarter of the camp's 45,000 prisoners died during Mirz's control. This sense of a 'line that should not be crossed' presumably went on to influence the later use of *deadline* to refer to a time limit or closing date in the early 1900s.

3. DOGSBODY

Dogsbody was originally an early nineteenth-century naval slang term for a basic, unpalatable meal of dried split peas boiled in a cloth bag, or else a similarly unappetizing concoction of watered-down biscuits flavoured with sugar or salt. Quite why such foods became known as *dogsbody* is unknown, but it has been suggested that the name may be a humorous reference to the smell of the food as it cooked, to the distended shape of the bag once its contents had been boiled or to its somewhat unpleasant taste. Whatever its origins may be, in the early twentieth century the word developed to come to be used by senior naval officers in reference to any junior officer or midshipman who was typically charged with carrying out lowly or unpleasant duties. This development probably came about simply through association with the negative connotations of 'dog', or else through use of the word 'body' to refer to a crew or group of men, but eventually led to the modern use of the word to refer to a drudge or similarly menial worker.

4. KIBOSH

The first recorded use of the word *kibosh* in English comes from Charles Dickens's *Sketches by Boz*, written in 1836, in which the phrase 'put the kye-bosh on' is used to mean 'do away with' or 'finish off'. The origin of the term is admittedly unknown, yet several explanations tracing the word back to a number of different languages have been suggested, ranging from Yiddish (in which it is popularly claimed that *kibosh* means a 'cheap price') to Scots (wherein *kye-boots* are shackles used to stop cows from straying too far away). Of all potential explanations of the word, however, a derivation from the Irish *caipín báis*, literally the 'cap of death' or the black cap worn by judges delivering the death penalty, is perhaps the most likely and the most unusual.

5. LEMUR

In Roman mythology, *lemures* were ghosts and ghouls who were said to wake at night to walk the earth, terrifying its inhabitants. The word variously described the malevolent, restless spirits of murderers and other criminals who had not been afforded a proper funeral or burial, or else the vengeful spirits of people who had died leaving unfinished business on earth. It was this ghostly description of the Roman *lemures* which in the eighteenth century led the Swedish naturalist Carl Linnaeus to apply the name first to a group of similarly night-dwelling species of loris native to south-east Asia, and ultimately to the larger nocturnal mammals of Madagascar that still bear the name *lemur* today. Although Linnaeus himself explained that he chose the name simply because the creatures' slow movements and nocturnal habits were reminiscent of the ghostly *lemures*, popular explanation claims that the name was intended to emphasize the ghostly appearance of the lemurs' wide-eyed faces, or else the eerie sound of their calls.

6. NIGHTMARE

Although it is used almost exclusively in modern English to refer simply to a bad dream – and ultimately, by extension, to any terrible situation or scenario – on its first appearance in the language in the fourteenth century the word *nightmare* originally described a female monster or succubus who was believed to sit on the chest of a sleeping person, causing a feeling of breathlessness or suffocation whilst they slept. In this context, the second part of the word is an Old English word used to describe a monster of this kind, *mære*, which is in fact one of the oldest recorded words in the entire language and dates back to the ninth century.

7. PANDEMONIUM

The word *pandemonium* has been used to refer to a clamorous state of confusion and chaos since the mid-1700s in English, although the creation of the word in fact dates from almost a century earlier. It was coined by the seventeenth-century English writer John Milton for use in his 1667 epic poem *Paradise Lost*, in which *Pandaemonium* is the 'Citie and proud seate Of Lucifer', and 'high Capital Of Satan and his Peers'; it is the capital city of Hell, the dwelling place of all demons and home of the central council chamber of all evil spirits. Milton coined the term from classical roots, combining the Greek prefix *pan-*, meaning 'all' or 'universal' (as in *panoramic* or *pandemic*), the Latin word *daemon*, and the Latin suffix *-ium*, used here, as it is in words such as *auditorium* and *stadium*, to indicate a location or setting.

8. PARAPHERNALIA

Formed from the Ancient Greek prefix *para-*, meaning 'beside', and *pherne*, meaning 'dowry', the word *paraphernalia* was originally a legal term used to refer to all the possessions of a woman – such as her clothes and jewellery – which remained her property after marriage and did not automatically pass over to her husband. In this context, the word was adopted from Roman family law in which a woman's *paraferna* comprised all of the items she held on to outside of any other assets that would instead constitute her dowry. By law, her husband could not use or sell any of these possessions without her permission, whilst she retained the exclusive control to bequeath them to others in her will rather than have them obligatorily pass to her spouse on her death. In English, the word first appeared in this context in the mid-seventeenth century before its use became more generalized, meaning simply 'possessions' and later 'necessary equipment', in the early 1700s. Due to the introduction of the Married Woman's Property Acts by Parliament in the late nineteenth century, the legal sense of *paraphernalia* has long since become obsolete.

9. PUNCH

As the name of a type of mixed alcoholic drink, *punch* dates from the early seventeenth century and was first adopted into English from the Hindi word for 'five', *panch*, as an original Indian *punch* contained just five ingredients: some type of liquor, water, lemon juice, sugar or molasses and spices. In this context, both *punch* and the Hindi word *panch* derive ultimately from the Sanskrit word for 'five', *pañca*.

10. ZOMBIE

In reference to a soulless reanimated corpse, the word *zombie* was first recorded in English in the early 1800s, although the image of a ferocious, bloodthirsty monster is a considerably more recent invention. The origin of the word in traditional voodoo sorcery, and in particular the traditional magic of the West Indies and southern United States, is fairly widely known: according to voodoo lore, a sorcerer or *bokor* can resurrect the dead either by taking control of and bottling a part of their soul known as the *zombi*, or else the body can be brought back to the life by a spirit, also known as a *zombi*, which enters the body to reanimate it. Like all voodoo culture, however, the word can ultimately be traced back to the traditional cultures of West Africa and is believed to be descended from the name of a snake-god, a supreme deity known as *Nzambi*, who is revered in the religion of the Bakongo people of northern Angola and Congo.

INDEX

271